# THE HEART STRANGELY WARMED

## The Chautauqua and Methodist Campgrounds at Plainville, Connecticut

## By Arthur K. Pope

Order this book online at www.trafford.com
or email orders@trafford.com

Most Trafford titles are also available at major online book retailers.

Cover Illustration: Th e Neuman family of New Britain, CT.
Grand Army Day, 1896, Plainville Camp Ground.

Print information available on the last page.

ISBN: 978-1-4120-8309-6 (sc)

*Trafford rev. 02/14/2019*

**Trafford**
PUBLISHING®  www.trafford.com
North America & international
toll-free: 1 888 232 4444 (USA & Canada)
fax: 812 355 4082

In the evening I went very unwillingly to a society in Aldersgate Street, where one was reading Luther's preface to the Epistle to the Romans. About a quarter before nine, while he was describing the change, which God works through faith in Christ, I felt my heart strangely warmed. I felt I did trust in Christ alone for salvation; and an assurance was given me that he had taken away my sins, even mine, and saved me from the law of sin and death.

John Wesley
May 24, 1738

# Foreword

I had never seen anything quite like the Plainville Campgrounds: the circles of toy-like gingerbread cottages, the tall trees, and the sense of quiet -- in spite of a busy road rushing by just outside the precinct -- all produced in me feelings of peace and well-being that must have been just what the campground's founders intended more than one hundred years earlier. I am descended from Methodist ministers and was raised in an active churchgoing family, but I was a suburban Methodist, a child of mid 20th century mainstream liberalism. Camp meetings and revivals were completely foreign to me. Only when I studied American church history did I come to appreciate the power of 19th century revivalism and the urge to go out into the wilderness and save souls. Arthur Pope has sketched the history of this movement, from the earliest days of Methodism in England to the present day, as seen in the development and preservation of one particular campground, founded by the New Haven district of the Methodist Episcopal Church.

This is a story that touches all Americans, even for those who do not practice Christianity or the type of Christianity that emphasizes individual conversion experience, for the heritage of camp meetings has shaped our nation. Evangelical Christians have been at the forefront of the abolition, temperance, and women's suffrage movements, along with a host of other efforts to improve the lots of those who lived at the margins of society. Even today, they continue to play an important and often powerful role in ongoing political and social debates. Some concentrate their efforts on reforming personal behavior, while others place a strong emphasis on working for social justice. Whether or not one agrees with them, understanding their concerns, the tradition they come from, and the language they speak is important to understanding and addressing their positions.

Camp meetings have shaped our society in other ways as well. The earliest ones were intended as religious affairs, but from the very beginning they also offered a rare chance to escape the day-to-day routine of work and consider the meaning and course of one's life. For city dwellers, the camp meeting offered a chance to escape to Nature. The sense of retreat to a place set apart for refreshment and renewal fed the gradual transformation of camp meetings first into the educational but less strictly religious Chautauquas and then into some of the first resort communities. Even secular resorts took their cues from the camp meetings. Plainville's tiny cottages represent a building type that was invented at camp meeting grounds but quickly became a model for vacation and resort cottages across the country.

While urban folk found respite in Nature, isolated farmers and frontier settlers found the opposite, a chance to escape from the demands of Nature and find the joys of human fellowship. Above all, camp meetings were and are communal events: the tiny, tightly-packed cottages with their wide-open front doors, the worship services, and the prayer and study meetings all force attendees to interact deeply with their neighbors. Not all the socializing has been in keeping with the aims of the organizers; an observer of the earliest camp meetings on the frontier wrote that "there were as many souls begotten as were saved." But to be part of something larger than oneself is a nearly universal human longing, and camp meetings help to satisfy that longing in more than one way.

This combination of Nature and Society lies at the heart of the camp meeting experience and at the heart of American society in general. For Ellen Weiss, chronicler of Wesleyan Grove on Martha's Vineyard, the campgrounds are an ancestor of American suburbs at their best: "societies of the like-minded, with strong family ideology, living in nature." (From *City in the Woods: The Life and Design of an American Camp Meeting on Martha's Vineyard,* Boston; Northeastern University Press, 1998, xviii)

In an era of metastasizing sprawl and four-car garages, when cell phones offer unlimited contact and DVDs and iPods offer uninterrupted entertainment -- always at a distance from other people -- the idea of spending time in a village of tiny cottages in the woods to rest, to commune with both nature and one's fellow humans, and to examine and perhaps alter the course of one's life all seems as impossibly quaint as the gingerbread trim that needs nearly constant repair and repainting. (On the other hand, what's rehab clinic for?) Places like the Plainville campground offer us a chance to escape, however briefly, our thing-ridden lives, to think about the things that lie beneath the surface, to slow down and recharge. Whatever our religious persuasion, or non-persuasion, these are values that nourish us.

Christopher Wigren, Deputy Director
Connecticut Trust for Historic Preservation

# Introduction

I like to write about people and places. To quote Thomas Wolfe, "We are the sum of all the moments of our lives. All that is ours is in them." I find this also to be true of places I have written about, whether it is the New Haven Green in Connecticut, Little Havana in Miami, or the Town House in Strafford, Vermont. The air in all of these places seems hallowed by the breath of other times.

What occurred at so many places lingers on the air, mixing with life in the present and giving strength for the journey to the future.

This book uses the present site known today as the Plainville Camp Ground Association in Connecticut to conjure up the past in order to try to begin to understand the great American religious and social movements of Methodism and Chautauqua. These movements enabled Americans to educate and revitalize themselves, allowing them to take courage in their 19th century lives to face the 20th century with utmost intelligence, reverence, and resolve.

Within its physical realm of tranquil grounds and unique architecture, the Plainville site allows us a close study of the restful and ennobling spirit of the past. We can draw inspiration from the strength this spirit exudes as we look to our own futures.

My hope is that this endeavor will serve to aid in preserving this spirit of the past for all to enjoy for all time to come.

Arthur K. Pope

# Dedication

This volume is respectfully dedicated to Harriet Barrett Eaton, matriarch and historian of the Plainville Camp Grounds.

Harriet Eaton at the campgrounds in 2004.

Collectively for over 100 years Harriet and her mother have carefully saved documents and photographs detailing the history of our American treasure. Over the last few decades Harriet has carefully researched and written a condensed history of the grounds that served as a basis for this volume.

Harriet Eaton at the campgrounds in 1922.

Married for over 50 years to the late Joe Eaton, Harriet is the mother of five children, an accomplished musician, church leader, and purveyor of civic leadership. Her feisty spirit warms our hearts as her life continues to this day to embody the exhortation of John Wesley: "Do all the good you can, by all the means you can, in all the ways you can, in all the places you can, at all the times you can, to all the people you can, as long as you can."

# THE HEART
# STRANGELY
# WARMED

# Chapter One:  John Wesley and the Rise of Methodism

To understand the camp meeting and Chautauqua movements in America, we must journey back to 18th century England where the church was facing a new challenge.

England was changing, and the churches were increasingly out of touch.  This was the time of Industrial Revolution.  Large and modern industrial cities were springing up mills, pits, factories, and chimneys belching smoke.  The established church, with its alliance of squire and parson, had little place in this new world.  Often in the new industrial city there were hardly any churches at all, and if there were, those living among the satanic mills would find that the old class-ridden churches had nothing to offer them.

The entire social structure was in need of revolution.  The wealthy upper classes and the self-satisfied middle class of skilled workers, shopkeepers, and merchants were getting rich from overseas trade, and they had embraced many of the reformed churches.  Beneath them, however, there was a vast throng of people who existed in a condition little above savagery.

These people were brutalized by a penal code and a prison system that staggers the imagination.  Adults and children could be legally hanged for 160 different offences, from picking a pocket for more than one shilling to snaring a rabbit on a gentleman's estate. Three out of four children of all

*Gin Lane* by William Hogarth

Perhaps more than any other artist, Hogarth depicts the debauched society of John Wesley's time. As described in *The Gospel in Hymns*, the painting illustrates the following:

(starting left middle and moving clockwise) Man and dog gnaw some bone. Carpenter pawns saw and coat at prosperous pawnshop owned by S. Gripe. Tattered woman pawns kitchen utensils to get drink. Parish beadle directs putting woman's body in coffin; her child crying on the ground. Drunken man impales a child on a spit. A house falls to ruins. Good house belongs to undertaker - sign of a coffin. In nearer house, barber hangs himself in a garret. Remaining good house owned by "Kilman," the distiller. In street two young girls from St. Giles Charity School are toasting one another. Two drunken beggars are fighting, crutch vs. stool. Drunken woman is carried off in a wheelbarrow while boy pours last glass down her throat. Mother gives baby a drink to keep it from crying. A peddler cries, "Buy my ballads and I'll give you a glass of gin for nothing." He has pawned his waistcoat, shirt and stockings; his body is a skeleton. Center, a diseased intoxicated woman takes snuff while baby falls to death over rail. Gin shop under street named "Gin Royal"; over door, "Drunk for a penny, Dead drunk for twopence, Clean straw for nothing."

classes died before their fifth birthdays. Church wardens who cared for the orphans and foundlings in the workhouses often took bastard children off their mothers' hands at so much per head, spent the money in frivolous living, and let the babies die. In one parish in Westminster, out of five hundred of such children received over a series of months, only one survived.

Harlotry and gin drinking flourished. The latter became a national curse and was responsible for much of the crime and a good deal of the poverty. In 1750 the consumption of this cheap drink was eleven million gallons! Drink was a popular business, and many of the gin manufacturers held high positions in the church and the state.

Add to these overwhelming factors the anvils of ignorance and illiteracy, and you have a degenerate picture. In the fifty years preceding the rise of John Wesley and his fellow evangelists, England reached its lowest pitch of moral degradation.

Into this climate came evangelical revival and at the center of it, John Wesley (1703-1791). Wesley was an Anglican clergyman with a dry, hard, priggish kind of faith. He went to America as a missionary with his younger brother Charles to serve as chaplain to the English colony at Savannah. There he refused to allow Nonconformists to receive communion and would not even read the burial service over their graves. If you want to get the feeling of this rather narrow individual, observe how he treated his girlfriend. When they were alone he read

John Wesley preaching at the Market Cross.

church history to her. After she jilted him, he responded by excommunicating her from the church!

Wesley did not stay long in Georgia. He was too straight-laced, too much a disciplinarian, and too lacking in tact. He was also victimized by females who found him attractive and whom he tried unsuccessfully to reform. Indicted by a grand jury on a number of foolish charges, he returned to England before the trial, hoping to lay his case before the colony's trustees.

This complete failure in his first encounter in the new world gave him such a jolt that he was led to search for a better religion than the one he had. He began to have doubts about his faith. All his fanaticism had not brought him inner peace. His religion seemed a burden, not a delight.

Wesley began to have encounters with the Moravian colony, which met in Aldersgate, London. In one of their meetings on May 24, 1738, he was converted, that is, had a deep emotional experience, which convinced him that what he thought were his sins were forgiven and that Christ and he now lived in a close personal relationship.

What follows is truly remarkable. For the rest of his life Wesley devoted himself to showing his discovery to the world. He began to think about those living outside the church in the desperate conditions we have described. Determined to reach them, Wesley began preaching not simply in churches, but to great crowds outside.

When John Wesley began to preach justification by faith alone and the experience of instantaneous conversion, Anglican churches

George Whitfield was hardly handsome, but as a preacher he was probably the most compelling religious presence in all of American history.

George Whitfield preaching out of doors.

closed their doors to him. Indeed, he was often attacked by mobs led at times by clergymen and even magistrates.

Field preaching began at Kingswood near Bristol with George Whitfield (1714-1770), a member of the Holy Club and charter member of the Methodist Group highly influenced by Moravians who emphasized conversion and holiness still common today to Methodism.

A persuasive orator, Whitfield went to Kingswood to present the Gospel to miners who were called "beasts of men," and later across England and America.

The Holy Club had been organized at Oxford and was led by Charles Wesley (1707-1788), brother of John. The group was aimed at deeper Christian experience and a life of Christian service. Because of systematic devotion and good works, members were derided with such names as Bible Bigots, Bible Moths, the Godly Club, and Methodists. The name that stuck was Methodists: "see with what method they do things."

Charles Wesley, known as a sweet singer and Gospel poet, was a giant in his own right. He was one of the great hymn writers of all time, composing 6,500 hymns found in the hymnals of all denominations today, including "Love Divine, All Loves Excelling," "Hark the Herald Angels Sing," "Christ the Lord is Risen Today" and "O for a Thousand Tongues to Sing." Largely through his influence, Methodism became a religion of song with its converts literally singing their message to the world.

John Wesley, who was an ordained minister of the Church of England, never disclaimed the holy orders of that church. However, in 1744 the first annual conference of the Methodist Episcopal Church was held and the articles of religion were drawn up. They were bound to a considerable extent upon the thirty-nine articles of the Church of England, but great emphasis was laid upon repentance, faith, sanctification, and the privilege of full, free salvation for everyone.

And so Wesley's great ministry began. Until he was 70 he traveled on horseback all over the country. It is estimated that he traveled 225,000 miles and preached 40,000 sermons. Shuttled back and forth over the lanes and turnpikes of England as leader of a spiritual revolution, he saved Britain from a duplication of the French Revolution. He visited from house to house with such constancy and zeal that he knew more about social conditions in his time than any of his contemporaries.

The genius of Wesley was that he listened to what the spirit was doing in the lives of ordinary people and made a theology out of it. He saw where people were and went out to meet them. Wesley died in London in 1791 and his life is best summed up in his own words:

*Do all the good you can*
*By all the means you can*
*In all the ways you can*
*In all the places you can*
*At all the times you can*
*To all the people you can*
*As long as you can.*

# Chapter Two: Methodism in the United States

John and Charles Wesley had visited America in 1735 as spiritual advisors to James Oglethorpe's colony in Georgia, but the actual beginnings of Methodism here came after 1766 when Philip Embury, a Wesleyan convert from Ireland, began to preach in New York and Robert Strawbridge started a congregation in Maryland. Francis Asbury (1745-1816) arrived in 1771. Born in Birmingham, England, where his parents were early followers of John Wesley, Asbury assumed leadership of the mere four Methodist workers already there.

While his colleagues favored a settled clergy located in populous areas, Asbury was convinced that preachers should go where the Gospel was most needed, exhorting his associates to "go into every kitchen and shop, address all, aged and young on the salvation of their souls." Asbury's desire to spread the Gospel kept him on the move the rest of his life traveling nearly 300,000 miles on horseback. He crossed the Appalachians more than 60 times and it is said of him that more people in the American countryside than any other person of his generation knew him.

Asbury's message in town and country emphasized God's free grace, humanity's liberty to accept or reject that grace, and the Christian's need to strive for perfection. He subordinated doctrine and church structures to the higher goals of communing with Christ and the faithful. His vision of Christianity reached beyond the inner life and called for social responsibility. Asbury argued strongly against slavery and urged abstinence from alcohol.

The first annual Methodist conference in America was held in 1773. In 1784 Thomas Coke, acting on authority from Wesley, proceeded with the organization of the Methodist Episcopal Church in America.

At the Christmas conference in Baltimore, Asbury and Coke were elected superintendents (and shortly thereafter styled bishops). The order of worship and articles of religion prepared by Wesley were adopted.

To say that Methodism grew rapidly due to these efforts is an understatement. The author has in his personal book collection original copies of the annual reports of the new church for 1795, 1802, and 1803. In 1795 it is reported that Methodism had grown to 48,121 whites and 12,170 blacks. Seven years later in 1802; 68,075 whites and 18,659 blacks. One can add a combined increase of 17,336 for the next year to get an idea of this movement's phenomenal

growth, which was to be significantly swelled by the camp meeting and revival phenomena of the years to follow, having far reaching consequences into the very life and soul of the nation.

Francis Asbury

# Chapter Three: The Rise of the Camp Meeting

*"True religion is a powerful thing –*
*a ferment, a vigorous engagedness of the heart."*

*Jonathan Edwards*

Following the American Revolution, interest in religion was on the decline with well under ten percent of the population belonging to local congregations. Religion had been dealt a strong blow by Deists, most notably Thomas Paine. His pamphlet, *The Age of Reason*, questioned traditional supernaturalism and was as widely discussed as his earlier condemnation of rule by the British.

Change, however, was on the way in the form of a religious revival that swept the country from the mid 1790s onward.

In the opening frontier a great awakening took place due to the work of Presbyterians and itinerants from Baptist and Methodist churches. In the east, Timothy Dwight, a grandson of Jonathan Edwards and president of Yale, lead the revival movement. A third of Yale's students were converted by religious revival and reform. Many of these students later promoted revival in New England, upstate New York and the west.

The revival spirit that transformed the beginning of the 19th century drew on the spirit of the American Revolution. Preachers called on individuals during this time, to exert themselves for God. Finding traditional churches largely irrelevant, they organized voluntary societies to lead the nation to reform, winning the lost and expressing the country's democratic spirit. It was during this period that the camp meeting was born.

While the origin of the camp meeting concept is somewhat obscure, historians have generally credited James McGready, a Presbyterian, with inaugurating the first camp meetings in 1799-1801 in Logan County, Kentucky. The camp meeting, a type of outdoor revival filled an ecclesiastical and spiritual need in the churchless settlements as the population moved west.

As the name implies, those who attended such gatherings came prepared to camp out, gathering at prearranged times from distances as great as 30-40 miles. Families brought bedding and provisions and pitched their tents around a forest clearing where log benches and a crude preaching platform constituted an outdoor church. As many as 10-20,000 people came to such meetings that were in constant session for 3-4 days.

People came partly out of curiosity and a desire for social contact and festivity, but primarily out of their yearning for religious worship. Activities included preaching, prayer meetings, hymn singing, weddings, and baptisms. A conversion experience was emphasized throughout, and shouting, shaking, and rolling on the ground often accompanied the tremendous emotional release that followed conversion.

There is little doubt that the rise of the camp meeting movement in America had a great deal to do with the prosperity of Methodism in the country. The entire focus of the camp meeting practiced the oral tradition of Methodism and reflected the revival sweeping the country. There was little concern with doctrine or intellectual analysis. For Methodists, camp meetings were formed in the tradition of Wesley to transmit the fire of the Scriptures through the spoken word and music.

On October 20, 1800, while itinerating through Tennessee, Bishop Asbury attended his first camp meeting and was deeply affected. He wrote the following in his journal:

> *The strand was in the open air embosomed in a wood of lofty beech trees. The ministers of God, Methodists and Presbyterians, united their labors. Fires blazing here and there dispelled the darkness, and the shouts of redeemed captives and the cries of precious souls struggling into life broke the silent midnight.*

Jesse Lee, an early Methodist leader, has left us another description of the early Camp Meetings, in his "History of the Methodists:"

> *We proceed in our religious exercises as follows: soon after the first dawn of day a person walks all round the ground in front of the tents, blowing a trumpet as he passes, which is to give the people notice to arise. About ten minutes after the trumpet is blown again with only one long blast, upon which the people in all their tents begin to sing and then to pray, either in their tents or at the door of them, as is most convenient. At the rising of the sun a sermon is preached, after which we eat breakfast. We have*

*preaching again at 10 o'clock and dine about 1. We preach again at 3 o'clock, eat supper about the setting of the sun, and have preaching again at candlelight. We generally begin these meetings on Friday and continue them until the Monday following about the middle of the day. I have known these meetings to continue without any intermission for two nights and a day, or longer; the people being continuously engaged in singing, praying, preaching or exhorting without any cessation. I have known some camp meetings to continue eight or ten days.*

1869 print of the Central Circle at the National Camp Meeting, Round Lake, New York.

The first of such gatherings in New England of which we have any account was at Haddam, Connecticut, in 1802. The preachers of the Middletown circuit assembled there, going down from the city by a vessel full-freighted with saints and sinners. A stand was erected in the center of a level piece of ground, and seats were provided for about one hundred persons. There were no tents or trees. Meetings at night, or when it rained, were

held in nearby houses or barns or on the vessel.
The meetings continued for three days and thirty
or forty people were reported to be converted amid
great demonstrations and fallings into catalepsy.
All of Middletown and its nearby villages were
moved when the vessel returned.

During the next two or three decades great
numbers of these camp meetings were held all over
the country but hardly ever in the same place.
They were inexpensive primitive gatherings
adapted to the poor people who frequented them.
At some central point in the Methodist circuit or
district where the owner of the ground or grove
was friendly and there was a good supply of pure
water and other conveniences, the widely scattered
people would come together, some in wagons,
some on horseback, some on foot. A plain shed-
like structure built of poles and a few rough boards,
served for a preacher's stand. Some logs with slabs
over them served as seats. Clean straw on the bare
ground with sheets and quilts upon it was made to
do for beds, and a partition of cotton cloth
separated the men from the women. A substantial
fire gave warmth by day and light by night.

Original speakers platform and crowd at Plainville, CT.

On Sundays, there were often congregations of thousands of hearers. Often roving drunken youth created disturbances. But the power of God frequently got hold of them, and the hand of the law, as a rule, proved efficient. The memoirs of all the early preachers are filled with accounts of these great gatherings and the triumphs of the gospel at them.

Following camp meeting at Somers, Connecticut in 1829, the word so spread in the surrounding regions that 130 people were converted and more than 100 joined the Methodist church. The usual way was that the new converts and the newly quickened believers were so filled with zeal that, on going home, they went to work at once for the salvation of their friends.

"Camp Meeting John Allen" encamped at Plainville, CT.

To the meeting held in the town of Industry, Maine, 1825, John Allen, then 30 years of age, went, as he used to say, "a bold blatant, rum drinking, fun-making Universalist, and came away a red-hot shouting Methodist." He died at the age of 92, on the East Livermore Camp Ground in 1887, having attended 374 camp meetings

By the mid 19th century, the camp meetings began to be held at more permanent locations. In the beginning, revivalists would arrive at one of these sites, rent a tent, dine and wash communally, and participate in religious meetings held in a clearing surrounded by tents. The oldest and perhaps largest of the permanent sites still in existence today is Wesleyan Grove in Oak Bluffs (named Cottage City until 1907), Martha's Vineyard, off the coast of Cape Cod, Massachusetts. Here in 1840 eight hundred people attended weekly meetings with two thousand people arriving for Sunday services. By 1858, over twelve thousand people were attending the Sunday meeting, making it the largest camp meeting in the world. The tents had evolved into canvas-topped, wood-sided, wood-framed, candlelit structures that glowed at night causing people to nickname all the religious ambiance the "Celestial City."

In 1859, the first elaborate Gothic cottage was prefabricated in Providence, Rhode Island, shipped to Martha's Vineyard and erected in three days. By 1864, forty tiny prefabricated Carpenter Gothic wooden houses had been constructed on their original tent platforms, sprinkled among 500 canvas and wood sided tents. Around this time, six local builders were prefabricating the cottages in

Avenue of Tents, Ocean Grove, N. J.

Above: 1908 Postcard showing Avenue of Tents in Ocean Grove, N.J. These tents are still in existence, and look very much the same today.

Below: Tents of the same style during the same period at Plainville, CT. These tents evolved into cottages in much the same manner as at Vineyard Haven and Ocean Grove.

quantity in nearby Edgartown on Martha's Vineyard.

Wesleyan Grove still glows today as the Celestial City. Although somewhat secularized, it still functions as a vibrant summer social community. Over the years it has evolved in prototypical fashion from that of the tents to a cottage with a larger room in the front, separated from a smaller room by a decorative arched partition. This second room contained a narrow stair that led to the upper sleeping level. Originally, kitchens and outhouses were separated from the cottages. During the early part of the twentieth century, small kitchens and bathrooms were added to the rear of the cottages.

In 1869, another significant Methodist camp meeting ground was started on the Atlantic coast in Ocean Grove, New Jersey. In 1894, the "Great Auditorium that seated over six thousand persons was completed. It became a symbolic center for a community that remains today committed to its religion and austere lifestyle. By the turn of the century a tent city with over 250 very distinctive innovative tiny tent buildings thrived.

The tents were built by the Association and leased to families for a full summer season. They consisted of a canvas-covered porch, and 11 x 14 canvas living-sleeping room and an 11x14 wooden section with kitchen, bath and dining area built behind the tent structure making a three hundred eight square foot structure.

Today one hundred fourteen of these dwellings still exist at Ocean Grove, many of them still being leased by their original families. There is a five-year waiting list for the use of these tents.

Also somewhat secularized, Ocean Grove thrives with thousands flocking to big name entertainment on Saturdays and big name religious speakers on Sunday. Because of its location on the shore, property values at Ocean Grove have soared to the millions.

Because these two camp meetings were located on the ocean shore, their survival as resorts was unquestionably assured whether or not they remained religious in nature.

## Chapter Four: Camp Meeting at Plainville, Connecticut

Visiting the old Methodist camp grounds at Plainville in the early 1990s, preservation architect Max Ferro pronounced it one of the finest surviving sites of its kind in New England, rating it higher than Wesleyan Grove at Oak Bluffs! Interestingly enough, the history of this surviving campground has remarkably paralleled the rise, success, and/or fall of campgrounds throughout the nation. Having looked at the background material, we are now ready to take a look at Plainville's remarkable history.

The earlier history of the Methodist meetings that later became known as the New Haven District Camp Grounds Association and its location is somewhat uncertain. Methodists near Milford, Connecticut, held meetings in a field in the early days of the Civil War. About this time they decided to remove inland to a location more central in the district.

In the years of 1863 and 1864, meetings were held at a site on the south side of Forestville in the town of Bristol, in a district known as Dublin Hill. This campsite was on the western slope of the hill near the junction of what is now Pine and Birch Streets.

In 1865, the meetings were transferred across the village to the north side of Forestville on Camp Street, the present site. Forestville is a village within the city of Bristol. Although located in

Plainville, the campgrounds, until recent times, were referred to as Forestville. Camp Street is actually the dividing line between Bristol and Plainville.

According to the civil engineer who named the grounds: "It will be a village in a forest and will be called Forestville." The grounds are located on the southern slope of a hill that is listed on the United States Geological Survey Map of 1889-90 as Campground Hill.

The committee that chose this spot had been commissioned to do so by the Presiding Elder, (now District Superintendent) of the New York East Conference of the Methodist Church in the New Haven, Connecticut, District. He wanted to find a central location for revival, presumably to capitalize on the religious fervor sweeping the land at that time.

Interestingly, some very well known businessmen served on that committee including Waldo Corbin of New Britain, founder of Corbin

One is hard pressed to identify this as the Camp Street of today, yet this is how the road appeared to the early settlers.

Lock Company, and John Sessions of Bristol, manufacturer of springs and known widely for his mechanical clocks. Both were Methodists.

The site chosen was farmland with beautiful views of the Bristol hills and a spring close by. In those early days a small section of the present area was rented for a one-day revival.

The people came on the appointed day in 1865 by oxcarts, farm wagons, lumber wagons and hay carts, bringing with them tents, bedding, baggage and food. They made a clearing in the trees, brush and undergrowth near what is now the present site of Camp Street and Northwest Drive.

Two years later, on June 28, 1867, a charter was granted by the Connecticut legislature for a corporation by the name of the New Haven District Camp Grounds Association.

From time to time extra plots of land were acquired. Among these was a right of way from Washington Street south to the railroad tracks where a small wooden structure known as Camp Station was erected. The station became a regular stop where campers would be met by wagons and various rigs and conveyed to the grounds. With the coming of the automobile, this train stop was discontinued and in 1928, the station land was sold to the New Britain Water Works.

In 1915, a five-acre lot was bought from farmer Oliver Robertson for $500. (The Robertson Family was active at the grounds for many years.) This plot of land is the present campus of the Gloria Dei Lutheran Church and is located on Camp Street directly across from the camp grounds. It was used as an athletic and recreational field and campfires were held there nights. It afforded a beautiful view of Connecticut's gently sloping hills. (Hard to imagine today.)

For many years the assembly was a tent colony, and thus received its name Camp Meeting.

From 1867 when the New Haven District Camp Ground Association was incorporated, until 1900, large tents were secured and erected. It was in these tents that the preparation, cooking and serving of food was made available to the people that came to camp meetings.

Concessions were let out and many other small tents were used for various purposes. There was one tent that was called the Oyster House, another was known as the Candy Store serving candy and ice cream. Barbers came, bringing their chairs with them, cutting hair and shaving in the open air. Local farmers provided food and produce of all types.

In those early days the water supply was secured from natural springs, located north of what is now Gladding Avenue. These springs were dug out, enlarged, walled up with stone and covered with heavy timber and planks. The area around the springs was fenced in. Just outside this enclosure a hand pump was installed where water could be obtained.

Protected kerosene lamps that were distributed about the grounds, fastened to the trees or set on posts, provided night lighting for the grounds. A regular lamp lighter was employed to clean, fill and lights these lamps. Tether lines were established at the north and south ends of the grounds where the horses could be cared for.

Situated where the present auditorium now stands, was a wooden building which housed the chairs that were used at the large assemblies. These assemblies were held in the open and the speakers spoke from an out-of-doors raised platform.

The Act of Incorporation and the first bylaws were recorded in 1891. There were twelve trustees and the Association consisted of one member elected by each quarterly conference of the Methodist Episcopal Churches in the New Haven District, and the members of the New York East Conference appointed to the churches in said district.

It was no simple organization. Committees included the following: Railroads, Music, Storage, Finance, Corporation House, Rental and Care of Cottages, Public Worship, Police, Lease of Tents and Sale of Lots, Audit, and Advertising. Bear in mind that although this was undeveloped rural wilderness, those in charge had to be ready to accommodate over 3,000 people at one time when the surrounding area perhaps only sustained a few hundred year round.

Coming from cities like New Haven and New Britain, these folks faced the challenges of urbanization and industrialization that left very little in the way of relief from the drudgery of work. There were few diversions for entertainment and emotional release, thus the huge popularity of the camp meeting.

Gradually the churches substituted houses for tents, and wood cottages were built by private individuals on a plot of land that they leased from the association. A plan was adopted for a speaking

stand in the center, now the Auditorium, with a
spacious circle area with a circumference of church
owned houses of similar style and size, including
one larger association building.

Radiating as spokes of a wheel from the outside
circle in the rear of the church houses were
avenues on which were built the residential
cottages owned by individuals. Later a larger outer
circle was added.

Soon after, an association building with guest
quarters and creature comforts for the clergy and
other dignitaries was completed. Individual
churches began constructing cottages on the
Circle. Eventually 24 -two-story cottages with
open sleeping quarters for men on one floor and
women on the other circled the platform.
Nineteen of these cottages remain today. Typically
these cottages, built on brick stilts with no
foundations, exhibited decorative lattice and stick
work on the porches and gable. Many had wide

The association building shown here on an old postcard
housed visiting dignitaries and guests as well as in later years
the communal showers. The building, now privately owned,
is little changed today.

double doors which, when open, served to encourage people to enter and join in the prayer meetings and to minimize the distinction between in and out of doors, emphasizing the open air communal nature of camp meetings. The circular arrangement and close proximity of the cottages also enforced the sense of community.

As time went on and the middle class became more affluent and had more leisure time, families began building the private cottages along the narrow avenues growing out of the circle. These cottages were generally one and a half or two stories tall, one room wide and two deep with a gable roof. In almost all a porch was incorporated forming a decorative focal point. Most were ornamented with decorative features loosely drawn from Eastlake, Stick Style, and Gothic Revival. Most of the remaining cottages date from the 1880s to 1910, and were not built to a high standard of structural integrity. It is a wonder that so many have survived into the 21st Century.

The Plainville camp meeting followed the national practice of Methodism's oral tradition of life transformation invoked by preaching and singing. By 1901, the year of the thirty-sixth Annual Camp Meeting, the phenomena had reached full maturity. The full program printed in this chapter outlines the whole remarkable schedule. Even more significant however, is the fact that with increasing free time allotted the middle class, the grounds began to be used all summer long by people in the private cottages as well as a number of related organizations and movements.

Among these was the American temperance movement, which held rallies on the grounds. This movement was strongly supported by the Methodists as an outgrowth of Wesley's struggles against alcohol a century before. Temperance remained a theme of Methodism well into the 20th Century.

On Sept 1, 1887, the Veterans' Plainville Camp Ground Association was organized "to carry on the brotherly, friendly feeling which had existed between the men during the Civil War, and to aid the veterans and their families, and to carry on the principles for which the Grand Army of the Republic stands." The Woman's Auxiliary, was organized in 1904. Rallies were held on the camp grounds until most of the veterans and spouses passed away. In 1939, these organizations were discontinued.

In 1902, the Camp Grounds Improvement Society was organized and for more than 25 years raised thousands of dollars to aid in beautifying and improving the usefulness of the grounds. That same year the Auditorium (still in use as a meeting area and picnic pavilion) was built. The committee appointed recommended it be built on the site of the preacher's stand and that it seat 1,000 people! Two plans were presented: the Octagonal and the Algier with the latter being unanimously accepted. A number of years later the auditorium was screened in to resolve a rather serious mosquito problem. These same screens were removed in the 1990s reportedly to save repair costs.

Also during this period it became evident that the old boarding tent had outlived its usefulness.

Before the building of the auditorium or tabernacle, as it was called by some, this preacher's stand with tent roof was the mainstay. Benches shown were placed in the new tabernacle and used until 2002 when they were removed to be replaced by picnic benches and plastic chairs.

Auditorium or tabernacle built in 1902 in the Algiers style, it could seat over 1,000 person and was often filled to overflowing.

In 1903-1904 the still-surviving John Wesley Dining Hall was built which included a screened in porch where food, such as sandwiches, pie, cake, ice cream and coffee were served over a counter. What really was fast developing was one of Connecticut's most popular country resorts. It was actually advertised as the "coolest spot in Connecticut" in brochures and postcards.

Soon many other denominations began to use the grounds. The new dining hall and auditorium were put to good use and accommodations at the Association Building and private cottages were strained.

For several years the Seventh Day Adventists held camp meetings on the grounds.

The Evangelical Free Churches more familiarly known as the "Scandinavians" used the grounds for many years for their annual Bible Conference or camp as it was sometimes called.

The Forestville Bible Conference Class, known as the Swedes, held their weeklong rallies for many years through the early 1980s. This group may, indeed more than any other, be responsible for the camp ground's present day survival, as we shall see later in this volume.

On Memorial and Labor Days hundreds of Methodist youths from Connecticut and New York converged on the camp grounds for religious observance and athletic meets.

But perhaps most famous of all, drawing crowds equal to the thousands who came to Camp Meeting, was the location of the Connecticut Chautauqua at Forestville on these grounds.

Only known photo of the original boarding tent at Plainville.

Early postcard of the John Wesley boarding house (built 1903-1904). Its appearance is little altered today.

Waitresses in the dining room of the John Wesley boarding house in 1906 (two years after completion). Tables shown were in existence and use until 2004 when they were unfortunately replaced by round modern tables. Otherwise the hall remains pretty much the same.

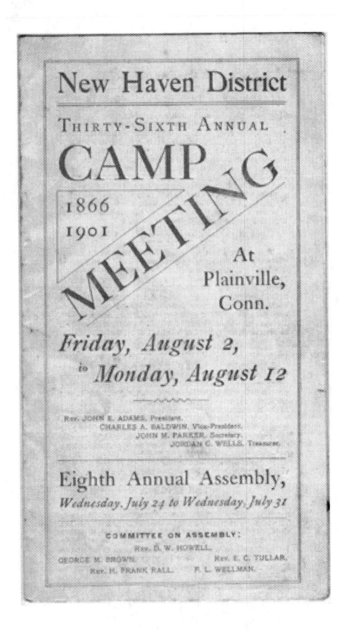

# New Haven District

## Thirty-Sixth Annual

# CAMP MEETING

1866
1901

At
Plainville,
Conn.

*Friday, August 2,*
to *Monday, August 12*

Rev. JOHN E. ADAMS, President.
CHARLES A. BALDWIN, Vice-President.
JOHN M. PARKER, Secretary.
JORDAN C. WELLS, Treasurer.

## Eighth Annual Assembly,

*Wednesday, July 24 to Wednesday, July 31*

COMMITTEE ON ASSEMBLY:
Rev. D. W. HOWELL.
GEORGE M. BROWN.          Rev. E. C. TULLAR,
Rev. H. FRANK RALL.      F. L. WELLMAN.

## THE CAMP-MEETING.

THE New Haven District Annual Camp-Meeting will be held upon the delightful grounds at Plainville, commencing Friday, August 2d ; closing Monday, August 12th. This Plainville Camp-Meeting has had a steady and prosperous growth for thirty-five years, and has become a great factor in the life and work of New Haven District Methodism. It is a genuine Methodist Camp-Meeting of the very best type, conducted on principles that commend it to the support of all people. The acquaintances formed by members of the various churches in the district at these annual gatherings are highly prized, and increases the interest the churches have in each other.

The whole encampment, including Camp-Meeting and Assembly, will be comprised within three weeks, and it is hoped that a large number of our people will be able to attend from the beginning to the close.

## TO THE PEOPLE.

The many friends who have met with us in former years will need no urging to come again. To all others we say, "Come with us, and we will do thee good." Let a multitude of newcomers test the charms of Plainville Camp this year ! You will find the Camp-ground in excellent order, all the surroundings neat and attractive, comfortable accommodations, good food at moderate expense, pure water ; and we shall hope, fine weather. Everything will be managed with the strictest regard for the comfort, enjoyment and benefit of all who attend.

## TO THE PREACHERS.

Dear brethren in the ministry, give your best endeavors to make this year's meeting more successful than any other ever held at Plainville. Call the attention of your people to it with earnestness and enthusiasm. Do this at once, and repeat the notice several times before the date of the meeting. Be sure to arrange to attend the meeting yourselves. The time at Plainville Camp will bring a wealth of recuperation to body, mind and soul. Pray for the meeting, and urge your people to come, especially the young people. They will have fine opportunities here for getting and doing good.

Furnished rooms at the Corporation House are provided for preachers at *one-half* of the regular rates.

## THE SINGING.

The singing will be conducted by Mr. W. M. Manchester, a competent leader, which assures us with excellent music. The Methodist Hymnal will be the standard book used at the Camp-Meeting. Those who have Hymnals will please bring them to the Camp-Meeting,—also the "Living Hymns" ; those who have not, can obtain them at the Secretary's office at a very low price. The new No. 3 Epworth Hymnal can also be obtained at the office.

FINLAY BROTHERS, PRINTERS, HARTFORD.

## THE HOUR OF PREPARATION.

The Hour of Preparation, which was a feature of such marked interest last year, will be continued, and in the same hands, this year. This meeting, beginning at 8.30 each morning and lasting till near the time for public service, will again be conducted by Rev. B. M. Adams, of Bethel, Conn. If this one service alone constituted the camp-meeting, it were well worth a journey to Plainville to attend it.

## EVANGELISTIC SERVICES.

The afternoon and evening meetings will frequently be followed by evangelistic services, at the stand or elsewhere, designed for the conversion of sinners, and the deepening of the spiritual life in believers. The Rev. Frank A. Scofield, of Meriden, will direct these services, and it is hoped ministers and laymen, young and old, will participate in them.

## THE VESPER HOUR.

This hour, each evening at 6.30, is under the auspices of the New Haven District Epworth League. It will this year be in charge of Rev. and Mrs. D.W. Howell, of North Church, Hartford, and not only the young, but people of all ages will find instruction and inspiration in these evening meetings.

## THE CHILDREN'S HOUR.

The Rev. A. L. Hubbard, of West Granby, assisted by competent helpers, will hold meetings for the children at convenient hours, which parents are earnestly exhorted to sustain by sending their children, and sometimes, as opportunity offers, by attending themselves.

## THE MINISTERS' RETREAT.

Rev. Benjamin M. Adams will occasionally meet the ministers on the ground for conference and prayer, with reference to the great responsibilities of the sacred office.

## BRING YOUR BIBLES.

Bring your Bibles to the Camp-Meeting, and bring a copy with you to every service—especially to the hour of preparation, and to the morning sermon.

## THE GRAND ARMY DAY.

The Grand Army Day, over which Mr. Charles A. Baldwin, of New Haven, President of the Veterans' Association, will preside, and for which a separate programme will be issued, will this year precede the Camp-Meeting, and will occur on Thursday, August 1. It is expected to be an occasion of unusual interest.

## CAMP-MEETING PROGRAM,
### Friday and Saturday, August 2 and 3.

---

### DAILY.

| | | | | |
|---|---|---|---|---|
| 6.00 a. m. | Rising Bell. | 1.30 p. m. | Children's Hour. |
| 7.00 " | Breakfast. | 2.30 " | Preaching. |
| 8.00 " | Family Worship. | 5.30 " | Supper. |
| 8.30 " | Bible Hour. | 6.30 " | Epworth League |
| 8.30 " | Tent Meetings. | 6.30 " | Tent Meetings. |
| 10.00 " | Preaching. | 7.30 " | Preaching. |
| 12.00 " | Dinner. | 10.00 " | Retiring Bell. |

---

# PUBLIC SERVICES.

---

### FRIDAY, AUGUST 2.

2 30  Opening Sermon,
Rev. Herbert Welch, *Middletown.*

6 30  Vesper Hour.

7 30  Sermon,
Rev. A. S. Hagarty, *Higganum.*

### SATURDAY, AUGUST 3.

8 30  Hour of Preparation.

10 00  Sermon,
Rev. Geo. M. Brown, *Derby.*

2 30  Sermon,
Rev. S. S. Lathbury, *Kensington.*

6 30  Vesper Hour.

7 30  Sermon,
Rev. A. P. Knell, *Essex.*

## CAMP-MEETING PROGRAM,
### Sunday, Monday and Tuesday, Aug. 4, 5 and 6.

### SUNDAY, AUGUST 4.

8 30  Hour of Preparation.

10 00  "The Great Duet."
        Address by Mr. H. H. Benedict, *New Haven.*

2 30  Sermon,
        Rev. Joseph Pullman, *Presiding Elder New York Dist.*

6 30  Vesper Hour.

7 30  Sermon,
        Rev. H. Frank Rall, *New Haven.*

### MONDAY, AUGUST 5.

8 30  Hour of Preparation.

10 00  Sermon,
        Rev. J. H. Knott, *Guilford.*

2 30  **Woman's Foreign Missionary Society.**
        Address by Mrs. Mary Scott Badley, *New York City.*

6 30  Vesper Hour.

7 30  Sermon,
        Rev. J. H. Lockwood, *Woodbury.*

### TUESDAY, AUGUST 6.

8 30  Hour of Preparation.

10 00  Sermon,
        Rev. B. P. Raymond, *Pres't Wesleyan University.*

2 30  **Our Missions in the Far East: Recent observations in India, China and Japan.**
        Address by Rev. Chas. H. Buck, *Tarrytown, N. Y.*

6 30  Vesper Hour.

7 30  Sermon,    Rev. H. C. Whitney, *Plainville.*

## CAMP-MEETING PROGRAM,
### Wednesday, Thursday, Friday, Aug. 7, 8 and 9.

### WEDNESDAY, AUGUST 7.

8 30   Hour of Preparation.

10 00   Sermon,
      Rev. Harvey E. Burnes, *New Haven.*

2 30   Sermon,
      Rev. W. M. Warden, *Southington.*

6 30   Vesper Hour.

7 30   Sermon,
      Rev. William M. Carr, *Hartford.*

### THURSDAY, AUGUST 8.

8 30   Hour of Preparation.

10 00   Sermon,
      Rev. G. S. Eldridge, *New Haven.*

2 30   Sermon,
      Rev. Alfred Hodgetts, *New York City.*

6 30   Vesper Hour.

7 30   Sermon,
      Rev. C. R. Pitblado, *Windsor Locks.*

### FRIDAY, AUGUST 9.

8 30   Hour of Preparation.

10 00   Sermon,
      Bishop W. F. Mallalieu, *Auburndale, Mass.*

2 30   Sermon,
      Rev. F. P. Tower, *Waterbury.*

6 30   Vesper Hour.

7 30   Sermon,
      Rev. Wm. McNicholl, *West Haven.*

# CAMP-MEETING PROGRAM,
## Saturday, Sunday, Monday, Aug. 10, 11 and 12.

### SATURDAY, AUGUST 10.

8 30  Hour of Preparation,

10 00  Sermon,
Rev. W. W. Winans, *Watertown.*

2 30  Sermon,
Rev. J. Howard Hand, *New Haven.*

6 30  Vesper Hour.

7 30  Sermon,
Rev. E. C. Tullar, *Seymour.*

### SUNDAY, AUGUST 11.

8 30  Hour of Preparation.

10 00  Sermon,
Rev. B. M. Adams, *Bethel.*

2 30  Sermon,
Rev. F. A. Scofield, *Meriden.*

6 30  Vesper Hour.

7 30  Sermon,
Rev. O. J. Range, *South Britain.*

### MONDAY, AUGUST 12.

8 00  Thirty-sixth Annual Love Feast.
Conducted by Rev. B. M. Adams.

### SWEDISH SERVICES.

On Saturday afternoon, July 20th, the *Swedish Camp-Meeting* will commence, under the auspices of the Swedish Camp-Meeting Association.

This meeting will continue through Saturday, Sunday and Monday, and will close with an early Love Feast on Tuesday morning at 7 o'clock.

# GENERAL INFORMATION.

The Swedish Meeting—July 20 to 23.
The Assembly—July 24 to 31.
The Grand Army Meeting—Aug. 1.
The Camp-Meeting—Aug. 2 to 12.

## THE BOARDING TENT.

The Boarding Tent will be in charge of a competent manager, Mr. M. E. Rogers, thereby insuring its guests an excellent table at very reasonable prices, as follows:—$1 per day; 5 days, $2.50; breakfast, 40 cents; dinner, 50 cents; supper 35 cents. Meats, vegetables, milk and groceries can be bought at the Boarding Tent at as low prices as are charged by local dealers.

Other parties, either Church societies, or private individuals are not permitted to furnish board or to sell meals, except to persons regularly belonging to their own tent's company.

## LODGINGS.

Good rooms can be obtained at reasonable rates by applying at the office. The usual price is 50 cents per day for a furnished room. Special rates for several days.

## RAILROAD SERVICE.

For Camp-Station from July 20 to August 13, Sunday excepted.

*Highland Division.*—Trains (steam) will stop at Camp-Station, same as heretofore; see local time-table for time of trains.

*Northampton Division.*—Trains for Plainville leave New Haven, a. m., 7.50; p. m., 12.04, 4.00, 5.57. Returning, leave Plainville for New Haven, a. m., 7.49, 10.55; p. m., 3.04, 6.55. Trains leave Plainville going north, a. m., 8.41; p. m., 4.00, 4.55, 6.55.

*Electric Third-rail Cars* from Hartford, New Britain and Bristol, stop at Plainville and Forestville, but not at Camp-Station. See local time table.

*The Electric Trolley* and Third-rail Cars connect with all trains stopping at Berlin for New Britain.

Round-trip tickets at reduced rates will be sold at the Railroad Stations.

Bus fare from Camp-Station to Camp-Ground, 10 cts.; from Plainville, 20 cents.

All baggage should be marked "Camp-Station," with owner's name.

Have letters directed: "Camp-Ground, Plainville, Conn." Inquire for, and mail letters at the Secretary's office. Stationery and postage can be obtained at the office. Oil can be bought until 5 p. m.

For any special information, write to JOHN M. PARKER, Sec'y, FORESTVILLE, until July 23d, after that date to PLAINVILLE, obtaining entry for July.

Early entrance to the grounds.

The automobile made it easier to get out to the Forestville countryside but indirectly contributed to the demise of the camp meeting as did talking pictures and radio, not to mention amusement parks and a host of other leisure time activities in the 1950s and 60s. A number of cottages were demolished to provide parking spaces for residents.

"Blest Be the Tie That Binds" -- Camp meetings would close on Monday mornings with a love feast and farewell circle.

Tranquil summer scene -- Meriden Avenue looking south around 1910. Note tent roof on cottage on left.

Original spring enclosure. At one point in this spring's history the water was bottled and sold commercially.

Gladding Ave with bridge to spring house.

The Spring House in more modern times. Note lantern to left. In 1910 water was piped to the Grounds from Bristol.

Mt. Olivet was an outdoor worship center to the north of what is now Gladding Ave. It was reached across a stone bridge, the ruins of which remain today. This bridge and a similar one up the avenue to the playground were built by Leon Gladding of the Glad Inn.

# Chapter Five: Chautauqua
## A Utopia For America

*"It has been the struggle of the world to get more leisure but it has been left to Chautauqua to show what to do with it."*

*President James A. Garfield*

In 1874 the population of the United States was approximately 44 million people. Americans were emerging from the grief of the Civil War and industry was growing.

Between 1860 and 1890 the country became one of the great manufacturing nations of the world, turning a largely rural society into an urban one. This meant a dramatic change in daily life, for on the farm there were no fixed hours and labor was unceasing with limited access to other people, new ideas, and any other entertainment.

In the city, on the other hand, there were defined hours of work and the stimulation of new ideas, new people and many venues for entertainment from pool halls to lecture halls. Into this newly found leisure time Chautauqua was born.

In August, 1873, Lewis Miller and John Heyl Vincent went to Fair Point Camp Meeting on Chautauqua Lake in New York to explore the possibility of creating what would become the Chautauqua Lake Sunday School Assembly, a program of lectures, sermons and music that evolved into the Chautauqua Institution. These two men were born within a few years of each other, but in their lives they really had only one thing in common—an interest in improving Sunday Schools.

In the early part of the nineteenth century, the Sunday School was a fairly new idea. It began as a place where children who worked in factories or in the fields six days a week came to learn reading, writing, and arithmetic. The Sunday School was the center of activity on a Sunday afternoon, and the children stayed for four or five hours. Their teachers were frequently public school teachers who were paid extra to teach on this day.

John Heyl Vincent was born in 1832, attended school for a few years, and then went directly into teaching himself. By 1850 he had decided to become a circuit preacher for the Methodist Church, traveling on horseback from parish to parish on a four-month circuit. Later he served churches in New Jersey and Illinois, ever dreaming that ministers and church school teachers should have a better education. In 1864 he found himself the editor of the newly formed *Northwestern Sunday School Teachers Quarterly* and later, editor of the Methodist publication, *The Sunday School Journal*.

Lewis Miller was born in 1829 in the new Ohio Territory. He loved the outdoors and was determined to make the farmer's life easier. Like Vincent, he had only a few years of formal education, and by the time he was sixteen he was teaching in a small school. It was as an inventor, however, that Miller became famous. He devised the Buckeye Mower and Reaper, which made him a rich man indeed, selling 8,000 a year out of Akron and Canton, Ohio, by 1863.

Miller's new found wealth enabled him to devote his time to other interests, one of which was the quality of the Sunday School in his Methodist Church. His first contribution to the Akron Methodist Church was a design for a new Sunday School. The plan included a large central hall, where the children could gather before and after their lessons, with many smaller rooms off the hall for classes. It was in this building at a national Sunday School Convention that the two men met

Chautauqua founders Lewis Miller (far left) and John Vincent (second from left) relax with others in New York in the later 1870s.

and formed the idea of the summer assembly.

In August of 1874, spurred on by massive publicity, people from 25 states and abroad jammed the old camp grounds with their persons and tents. These were Christians of all denominations.

The week began with a devotional service that included a reading of Old Testament verses and the singing of "Nearer My God To Thee." The programs the rest of the week were instructional. Although there were eight sermons, there were twenty-two lectures on the theory and practice of Sunday School work and seven lectures on such topics as Biblical history and geography. At the end of the two weeks, people gathered in a large tent and took a written examination of fifty questions on the Bible and other studies, and 152 of them received diplomas.

The resort atmosphere was enhanced with evening concerts on the lake and choral concerts under trees bedecked with Japanese lanterns.

On August 10, 1878, John Vincent announced the formation of the Chautauqua Literary and Scientific Circle (CLSC). It was to be a four-year course of home reading with a certain number of books to be read each year loosely following academic themes and disciplines. He announced that CLSC was for busy people who left school years ago as well as those who never went to high school. The circle welcomed mechanics, mothers, farmers, and people of leisure and wealth who did not know what to do with their time. By 1891, 180,000 people had enrolled and 12 percent completed the course. 800 people graduated at

Chautauqua in 1882 and by the 1920s, 300,000 had enrolled.

Original Chautauqua (NY) in 1817. Poles held flaming torches for night meetings. Note the striking similarity to Plainville, CT.

Two other programs grew out of Chautauqua in its first fifty years. Independent Chautauqua Assemblies emerged across the country, which were usually settled summer communities with an open-air pavilion or tabernacle, dining halls and cottages. By 1904 there were nearly 300 such assemblies booking prominent speakers and luring large crowds. But in the face of the movies, the automobile, and the radio, and without the substantial financial resources and loyalty of the parent institution, almost all of these programs failed by 1930. Some like that at Plainville, Connecticut, lasted into the 1950s, and 25 others survive today.

In 1907, Keith Vawter, a partner in the Redpath Talent Bureau, created a traveling tent show known as the Chautauqua Circuit which would travel about the country much as a circus does. It included teachers, preachers, scientists, explorers, statesmen, politicians, yodelers, whistlers, you name it! The contract system and traveling arrangements made the circuit profitable from about 1910 through the late 1920s. In its peak years there were more than one hundred traveling shows and upward of ten million tickets sold in a single summer.

The parent organization survives to this day with its quaint Victorian cottages and revitalized million-dollar real estate. It continues to be visited by presidents and world leaders, scientists, explorers, pianists, choirs, opera and the biggest lecture and entertainment names the world has to offer. It is a mecca for persons of all religious faiths.

The Connecticut Chautauqua at Plainville/Forestville grew into one of the largest and most popular in the nation attested to by the 1901 program and other ephemera that follow. Until the 1950s the Connecticut Chautauqua attracted thousands to Plainville to hear speakers of national prominence, continue work on their home reading courses, learn many new skills such as cooking, and relax amidst the beauty of rural Connecticut.

HARTFORD, May, 1911.

*Dear Friend:*

The Chautauqua Assembly at Plainville, July 22—August 1, is to be of unusual interest this year. Aside from the many varied attractions, we are laying special emphasis upon *The Sunday School Work.* At a considerable expense the Committee has secured the services of three leading experts, two of whom have a national reputation. From Sunday, July 23, until Thursday, Dr. Wade C. Barclay, of Chicago, Educational Director of the Board of Sunday Schools of the M. E. Church ; Thursday until Sunday, Mrs. J. W. Barnes, of New York, also employed by this Board ; Monday and Tuesday, Mr. Oscar A. Phelps, Superintendent of the Sunday School of the great Center Church, Hartford. These will speak twice each day on technical Sunday School work — 8:30-9:45 a.m., 5:00-6:00 p.m. Thus at your very door is put the best there is to be had. For the sake of your school, for your own sake and the encouragement of the Committee and speakers, will you not support a part at least of the Assembly ? If you desire a program, send to B. F. Gilman, 137 Jefferson Street, Hartford.

Recognition Day, August 1. Booker T. Washington is to be the speaker.

**1911 postcard invitation to the Plainville Chautauqua Assembly. Note Booker T. Washington as speaker.**

As in New York a recognition for graduates of the four year course of home reading was held. Graduates at Plainville marched through the grounds behind a class banner to a golden gate for the ceremonies. Small children dressed in white led the way to the diploma awarding ceremony. Note the white canvas around the auditorium (below). Admission to all Chautauqua events was by season ticket.

Until shortly after the Second World War, cooking classes were popular at the Connecticut Chautauqua. This photo shows the 1910 cooking class on the steps of the Chautauqua cottage.

The Home Reading class gathered at Plainville. 10,000 such circles were established in the first twenty years a quarter of them in villages with a population of less than 500. There were even a number in prisons.

This original Plainville Chautauqua Literary and Scientific Circle symbol is now in the possession of Harriet Eaton who rescued it from a trash pile headed for the dump.

Many a pageant entertained Chautauquans. Judging from the costumes, this one must have been pretty exciting.

# ᵗ THE ᵗ

# CONNECTICUT

# CHAUTAUQUA

## ASSEMBLY

## AT PLAINVILLE, CONN.

### JULY 24-31, 1901

### THE COMPLETE PROGRAM

Press of The Waterbury Blank Book Mfg. Co.

REV. JOHN E. ADAMS, D. D.
*President of the Board of Trustees.*

## The Assembly Idea

The thought of combining recreation with something that shall give mental stimulus is becoming the popular way of passing the summer vacation. It is not laziness that the hard worked man or woman needs, but a restful change of occupation that will bring new ideals and impulses. The Assembly idea offers the most feasible and inexpensive method of satisfying this need. The lectures, the music, the entertainments, the social enjoyments of the Chautauqua Assembly, the life under the magnificent forest trees, listening to the songs of birds, or if one will, stealing away into the dark shade of the woods, relaxing every nerve and muscle, and rest and *rest* and REST—these things build up brain and body and send one back to work with renewed strength and courage.

## The Assembly

The Assembly is a Summer Lyceum with the best lectures, concerts, and entertainments, a summer school with competent instructors, a summer resort for recreation, with advantages for social, intellectual, and spiritual benefits of the highest order. It offers something good and helpful and interesting every hour of the day from 8:30 A. M. to 10 P. M. The program has been prepared at considerable expense and with much careful thought and labor, and it is confidently expected that it will be duly appreciated and loyally supported by those who will be glad to see a Chautauqua Assembly established in Connecticut.

# Official Program

OF THE

# CONNECTICUT
# CHAUTAUQUA ASSEMBLY

AT

# PLAINVILLE, CONN.

## JULY 24-31, 1901

### ASSEMBLY ASSOCIATION

D. W. Howell, *President.*
Hartford.

G. M. Brown, *Supt. of Instruction.*
Derby.

H. Frank Rall, *Treasurer.*
New Haven.

E. C. Tullar, *Supt. of Gates*
Seymour.

F. L. Wellman,
New Haven.

### BOARD OF TRUSTEES

J. E. Adams, New Haven.
J. M. Parker, Hartford.
C. A. Baldwin, New Haven.
T. H. Coe, Hartford.
M. W. Terrill, Middletown.
B. B. Savage, New Haven.
D. J. Clark, Meriden.
N. A. Fullerton, New Haven.
J. C. Wells, Hartford.
T. Levitt, Bristol.
I. A. Spencer, Waterbury.
C. H. Jorey, Seymour.

### Rev. Jesse Lyman Hurlbut, D. D.

**Rev. Jesse Lyman Hurlbut, D. D.**

Dr. Hurlbut has been identified with the Chautauqua movement from its inception and has many times appeared upon the platform of all the prominent assemblies in this country. His rare ability as a Normal Class instructor is fully demonstrated in the fact that for more than fifteen years he has had charge of this department at the Original Chautauqua and will begin his work there this season immediately after our Assembly closes. The six hours that will be under his direction will be greatly appreciated by all interested in Sunday School methods. Dr. Hurlbut will also give some lectures and deliver the Recognition Day address. He is one of the Vice-Presidents of the C. L. S. C. class of '82, the famous "Pioneers," and has always been an enthusiastic Chautauquan. It will be a pleasure for Connecticut Chautauquans to meet him and for the class of 1901 to receive their diplomas from his hands.

### Miss Frances Walkley

Miss Walkley is a thoroughly trained professional Bible Student and normal worker. She is a graduate of the Springfield Bible Normal College, which is to be affiliated with the Hartford Theological Seminary. She is now a salaried worker on the force of the United Congregational Church of New Haven, as well as leader of the New Haven Primary Union.

### Mrs. V. E. Keeler

Mrs. Keeler is the Vice-President for Connecticut of the National Household Economic Association and will conduct the "Woman's Hour." Her discussions are upon topics of great interest to every woman who is ambitious to be a model home keeper. The work of the Women's Clubs is rapidly turning to a practical consideration of Domestic Science as one department of its study and this is the subject that will be given most emphasis at the Woman's Hour meetings.

### State Senator Franklin R. Burton

Senator Burton is a man that has won his way to the confidence and esteem of his fellow citizens through strict fidelity to public trust. His regard for every good enterprise induces him to lay aside his business and official burdens for the day that he may identify himself with the interests of the Connecticut Chautauqua Assembly. The management considers itself honored in securing this man to introduce the Governor.

### Rev. J. Benson Hamilton

Dr. Hamilton has been a pastor in prominent churches in Brooklyn and is now President of Walden University, Nashville, Tennessee. His lecture, "Aladdins Lamp in the Sunny South," is descriptive of scenes and sights among the colored people, giving their home life, surroundings and struggles for better things. The lecture is illustrated by a choice selection of stereopticon views.

# COMPLETE PROGRAM

OF THE

# Connecticut Chautauqua Assembly

HELD NEAR

## PLAINVILLE AND FORESTVILLE
### CONNECTICUT

## July 24th to 31st, inclusive, 1901

❦

## Wednesday, July 24

*OPENING DAY.*

AFTERNOON.

2:30—OPENING EXERCISES. Music. Short addresses by Rev. D. W. Howell, Rev. G. M. Brown, Rev. J. L. Hurlbut and others, outlining the purpose and work of the Assembly.

4:00—C. L. S. C. RALLY SERVICE. All Chautauquans upon the grounds are requested to be present, exchange greetings, become acquainted, put on the colors.

5:00—ORGANIZATION OF THE ASSEMBLY CHORUS, conducted by George Waldo Lackey. It is desirable that as large a chorus as possible shall begin its work at the opening of the session.

EVENING.

7:30—MUSIC.

8:00—STEREOPTICON LECTURE, "THE ALADDIN'S LAMP OF THE SOUTH." Rev Jay Benson Hamilton, D. D., of Nashville, Tennesee.

This lecture is profusely illustrated with views of southern life and will be full of entertainment as well as instruction.

Mr. Theodore H. Miller of Waterbury, Stereopticon Operator, will have charge of the Stereopticon Work during the Assembly.

### Governor George P. McLean

Connecticut Day could not be more honored than in having as its orator the chief executive of the State. This day should attract thousands to the Assembly. It is really the day of the establishment of Chautauqua Assembly work in the state and should be recognized as the inauguration of a movement that may have great influence upon the civic, the social, and the intellectual life of the commonwealth. The Governor's staff and many state officials are expected to be present. The day will be made merry with music, stirring speeches, and Connecticut good will. Last year more than one hundred of these Assemblies were held in the different states in the Union and with their helpful influence reached literally millions of people. This year for the first time Connecticut joins in the promotion of what has become the most popular educational movement this country has ever known.

Gov. Geo. P. McLean

### United States Senator Orville H. Platt

Senator Platt is sufficiently well known in his state to guarantee his popularity as the speaker for the evening of "Connecticut Day." Whenever he can be induced to take the platform, his utterances are always received with profound interest and he never fails to add new laurels to his already splendid reputation as an orator. His long and honorable career in the United States Senate has won for him the universal regard of his fellow senators and when it is known that he is to speak upon some question pertaining to important legislation the Senate Chamber and galleries are filled. His conservative position concerning the declaration of war with Spain, and his most earnest support of the country's cause after war had been declared, brought him the universal commendation of the nation. And the wisdom more recently shown as chairman of the committee on Relations with Cuba gives him foremost rank among the ablest legislators of the times.

### The General Assembly Approves

The State Senate and House of Representatives on the third day of June unanimously adopted the following resolutions:

"Inasmuch as the twenty-fifth day of July, 1901, has been duly set aside as "Connecticut Day" by the Connecticut Chautauqua Assembly, and as His Excellency, Governor George P. McLean, the Hon. O. H. Platt, United States Senator from this state, and Hon. Franklin R. Burton, senator from the Seventh District, have accepted invitations to be present and address the Assembly upon said day, therefore.

Be it resolved, that this General Assembly do by this act express its approval and gratification by joining the said Connecticut Chautauqua Assembly in officially naming said day, and further,

Be it resolved, that the members of this General Assembly do, in so far as their interest and pleasure shall permit, attend and enjoy the exercises on the said "Connecticut Day" at Plainville, July 25, 1901.

# Thursday, July 25

## CONNECTICUT DAY.

### MORNING.

8:30—CHAPEL SERVICE. Conducted by Rev. W. W. Winans.

9:00—CHAUTAUQUA NORMAL CLASS. I. "Old Testament History." Dr. J. L. Hurlbut.

JUNIOR CHORUS. Drill conducted by Mr. Lackey.

10:00—CHURCH CONGRESS. Opening session. Topic: "The Mission of the Modern Church. How it is being fulfilled. Opportunities for more efficient work." Address by Rev. J. E. Adams, D. D., followed by general discussion.

JUNIOR NORMAL CLASS. Conducted by Miss Frances Walkley.

11:00—LECTURE. Rev. H. Frank Rall, Ph. D., "Paul and His World."

### AFTERNOON.

1:30—WOMAN'S HOUR. Topic, "Household Economics." Discussion conducted by Mrs. V. E. Keeler.

2:00—BAND CONCERT. Plainville Military Band.

2:30—ADDRESS. By His Excellency, Geo. P. McLean, Governor of Connecticut. Address by Rev. John E. Adams, D. D., introducing State Senator Franklin R. Burton.

4:00—CHAUTAUQUA ROUND TABLE. Reports from Circles. The work in Connecticut.

5:00—ASSEMBLY CHORUS DRILL. Conducted by George Waldo Lackey.

### EVENING.

8:00—MUSIC BY THE PLAINVILLE MILITARY BAND. Address by United States Senator Orville H. Platt.

It is at considerable personal inconvenience that Senator Platt has made it possible to be present at the Assembly on Connecticut Day. He should receive a royally enthusiastic greeting in appreciation of his willingness to honor us with his presence on this occasion.

## Mr. George Waldo Lackey

Mr. Geo. Waldo Lackey

The work of the Assembly would not be complete without chorus drill for both adult and unchanged voices. Mr. Lackey has been engaged to conduct this work; he has gained an enviable record as a musical director in church choirs, public schools, and large choruses, and is eminently fitted to take this position at the Assembly. He also has considerable reputation as a composer of children's songs, having recently written the words and music to a song cycle entitled, "In Days to Come," which has been rendered with charming effect by a chorus of children. The junior chorus will take great delight in its work each morning and it is desirable that a strong chorus of adult voices shall be formed for the five o'clock hour each afternoon. Mr. Lackey will direct the two evening concerts and the juniors' afternoon concert; also do some solo work during the Assembly.

## Mr. John E. Lewis

Mr. Lewis is not only a successful business man, but is an example of what a man can do along some special line of research. His greatest pleasure as a pastime is a combination of photography and astronomy. He has the distinction of being the first man in this country to photograph a meteor in its flight, an interesting account of which he gives in his lecture. This lecture will be illustrated with about seventy slides, many of them being original negatives made in recent years at different observatories, showing the actual appearance at the time of making the photograph, of comets, meteors, star clusters, nebulae, the moon in its various phases, etc.

# Friday, July 26

---

*TEMPERANCE DAY.*

---

### MORNING.

8:30—CHAPEL SERVICE. Conducted by Rev C. G. Clarke.

9:00—CHAUTAUQUA NORMAL CLASS. II. "The Old Testament World." Dr. J. L. Hurlbut.
Junior Chorus Drill by Mr. Lackey.

10:00—CHURCH CONGRESS. Topic, "Choirs and Their Music." Address by Waldo S. Pratt, Mus. D., Professor of Ecclesiastical Music in Hartford Theological Seminary.

General discussion.

JUNIOR NORMAL CLASS, conducted by Miss Frances Walkley.

11:00—LECTURE. The Bible in Recent Light. Rev. H. S. Scarborough.

### AFTERNOON.

1:30—WOMAN'S HOUR. Topic, "Woman's Work." Discussion conducted by Mrs. V. E. Keeler.

2:30—PLATFORM MEETING. "Temperance Teaching in the Schools." Mrs. Forbes, President of the State W. C. T. U. will speak. Several prominent teachers will discuss the "Best Methods"

4:00—CHAUTAUQUA ROUND TABLE. "What a Chautauqua Circle can do for a Community." Short address by Rev. W. S. Sheldon.
General discussion, C. L. S. C. Council.

5:00—ASSEMBLY CHORUS DRILL. Conducted by George Waldo Lackey.

### EVENING

7:30—MUSIC.

8:00—STEREOPTICON LECTURE "The Heavens Above." Mr. John E. Lewis.

This lecture will include some of the finest results of astronomical photography, and it is expected that these with the aid of a superior stereopticon and a description by the speaker without technical details, will make the lecture not only instructive but entertaining.

9

### Major George A. Hilton

Major Hilton possesses rare ability as a popular lecturer. Few, if any, surpass him in pleasing and profitable address. The *Cincinnati Enquirer* says: "Major Hilton as a thinker and orator is strong and clear, possessing wonderful magnetism over his audience. In every respect he is the equal of, if not superior to, the late John B. Gough. He is eloquent and forcible with a delicate humor that is irresistible." Another press notice says: "On the platform he is entirely at ease and enters into his subject with the vim

Major George A. Hilton

and earnestness of a born orator. His intense enthusiasm and earnest convictions, coupled with a knowledge of the right thing to say and how to say it, make him a power upon the platform."

### Rev. D. Stuart Dodge, D. D.

It is a valuable addition to our program to be able to announce that Dr Dodge has kindly consented to be one of our eleven o'clock lecturers. He is President of the Presbyterian Board of Home Missions. He has travelled extensively through the Far East and is interested to an enthusiastic degree in all educational questions concerning Syria and Egypt. He was at one time President of Beirut college and continues his interest in that institution. A most interesting and instructive lecture may be anticipated.

# Saturday, July 27

*EVERYBODY'S DAY.*

### MORNING.

8:30—CHAPEL SERVICE, conducted by Rev. W. D. Tuckey.

9:00—CHAUTAUQUA NORMAL CLASS. III. "New Testament History." Dr. J. L. Hurlbut.

Junior Chorus Drill, conducted by Mr. Lackey.

10:00—CHURCH CONGRESS. Topic, "If the Pulpit does not reach men as formerly, why not? Why are not the masses more in sympathy with the church? Is the fault in pulpit or pew?"

Addresses by Rev. Louis H. Holden and Mr. Noel H. Jacks, followed by general discussion.

Junior Normal Class conducted by Miss Frances Walkley.

11:00—LECTURE. "Education in Syria and Egypt." Rev. D. Stuart Dodge, D. D.

### AFTERNOON.

1:30—WOMAN'S HOUR. Topic, "What is a Home?" Discussion conducted by Mrs. V. E. Keeler.

2:30—MUSIC.

LECTURE. "Character as Capital." Major George A. Hilton.

4:00—CHAUTAUQUA ROUND TABLE "Books a Bane or Blessing." Short address by Mr. Robert E. Platt. General Discussion, C. L. S. C. Council.

5:00—ASSEMBLY CHORUS DRILL. Conducted by George Waldo Lackey.

### EVENING.

8.00—Grand Concert.

### Rev. H. S. Scarborough

Rev. H. S. Scarborough, who lectures on "The Bible in Recent Light," is a graduate of Yale College and Yale Divinity School. He has already demonstrated his ability in this line by previous lectures on Old Testament subjects, which have been marked by thorough scholarship and attractive presentation.

11

### Rev. John E. Adams, D. D.

It required considerable persuasion to secure the consent of Dr. Adams to appear upon the Assembly program, but it is cause for general congratulation that he did so adjust his plans that he can give the opening address of the "Church Congress," and also preach at eleven o'clock on Sunday morning. The pulpit and platform ability of Dr. Adams is equalled by few in his own or any other denomination.

### Rev. Rockwell Harmon Potter

The Rev. Mr. Potter of Hartford is a young man of unusual promise and power. He has been but three years in the ministry. For two years he was pastor of the Dutch Reformed Church at Flushing, L. I. There his success was so notable that he was considered for several prominent pulpits, including that made vacant by the death of Dr. Storrs. He finally accepted a call to the old historic Center Church of Hartford.

### The Church Congress

It is expected that the ten o'clock hour each morning will be very popular and profitable. The questions to be discussed are those that should interest every person in any way connected with church work. It is hoped that all who attend will freely take part in the general discussions. A question box for queries relating to the church will be one of the features of the hour. This interchange of thought by men of all denominations cannot fail to increase interest in the work of the church and to foster the spirit of fraternity among them The Chautauqua movement is entirely undenominational and the Church Congress seeks to emphasize this fact.

### Sunday School Work

The first Assembly was held at Chautauqua, N. Y., in 1873, and was planned particularly for Sunday School workers. No real Chautauqua Assembly ever loses sight of this important work. The department of Bible Study for both adults and juniors will be full of interest for old and young. The Sunday School teacher that can be in Dr. Hurlbut's classes for a week cannot fail to receive inspiration for the work. Miss Walkley is one of the most efficient and successful workers among the younger classes that can be found. Mr. W. H. Hall, the President of the State S. S. Association, Dr. J. L. Hurlbut, and other Sunday School workers, will speak on S. S. Day, when questions of vital interest to the work will be discussed. The lectures by Dr. Rall and Rev. H. S. Scarborough will be of interest to Bible students and teachers.

### C. L. S. C. Round Tables

The Chautauqua Literary and Scientific Circle Round Tables will be centers of interest to all Chautauquans. Reports from circles will be called for, short addresses given concerning the work, and plans discussed for circles and the readings of the coming year. The Chautauqua books for next year's work will be on sale. The class of 1905 will be organized. This Assembly is to be the center of C. L. S. C. operations in Connecticut and representatives will be in attendance from every part of the state. Every Chautauquan that comes upon the grounds is requested to report and register at C. L. S. C. headquarters.

# Sunday, July 28

MORNING.

9:00—PRAISE AND PRAYER SERVICE.

9:30—SUNDAY SCHOOL.

10:30—DEVOTIONAL SERVICE. Sermon by Rev. John E. Adams, D. D., Presiding Elder of the New Haven District of the New York East Conference.

AFTERNOON.

2:30—SONG SERVICE. Assembly Choir.
Sermon by Rev. Rockwell Harmon Potter, pastor of the Center Congregational Church, Hartford, Conn.

EVENING.

7:30—CHAUTAUQUA VESPER SERVICE.
Sermon by Rev. Harold Pattison, pastor of the First Baptist Church, Hartford, Conn.

## Sabbath at the Assembly

Sunday will be a day of rest and worship. The gates will be open, no admission fee asked, but a silver offering requested at each of the preaching services during the day.

The management will insist upon the strictest observance of order upon the grounds in accordance with proper regard for the day.

The boarding houses will be open, but all other places of business will be closed. People are requested not to come with the purpose of making it a day of pleasure, but that they may attend divine worship in the same spirit in which they would be found in church.

## Rev. Harold Pattison, D. D.

Dr. Pattison, pastor of the First Baptist Church of Hartford, is one of the strong, popular speakers of the state. His coming to our Assembly platform to deliver the Sunday evening sermon is greatly appreciated and renders the service especially attractive to those who can avail themselves of the opportunity of hearing him.

### Mrs. Mary Scott Badley

Mrs. Mary Scott
Badley

The management considers itself very fortunate in securing this charming woman for two of her illustrated lectures upon India. For twenty years she lived and traveled in that land with both eyes open, and is beyond question the best informed and most eloquent woman upon the platform, who lectures upon that exceedingly interesting country of the Orient. The trees, the birds, the flowers, the hills, the mountains, the huts, the dirt, the moral degredation, the domestic, the social, the religious life, the mosques, the temples, the tombs, the cities, are all called upon to pay tribute to her skill in weaving them into her lectures with charming effect. The views she presents upon the screen are not of the hackneyed sort. Many of them have been prepared by her son who is now in India. Mrs. Badley also gives one eleven o'clock lecture.

### Rev. H. Frank Rall, Ph. D.

Rev. H. Frank Rall, Ph. D., who gives two lectures on Paul, is pastor of Trinity M. E. Church, New Haven. Dr. Rall is a recent graduate of Yale University. As Hooker Fellow of Yale he spent two years of study abroad, taking his degree of Doctor of Philosophy at the University of Halle.

# Monday, July 29

---

*SUNDAY SCHOOL DAY.*

---

### MORNING.

8:30—CHAPEL SERVICE. Conducted by Rev. H. C. Whitney.

9:00—CHAUTAUQUA NORMAL CLASS. IV. "The New Testament World." Dr. J. L. Hurlbut.

Junior Chorus Drill, conducted by Mr. Lackey.

10 00—CHURCH CONGRESS. Topic, "The Relation of the Sunday School to the Church. By what means can it be made more of an open door to Church Membership." Address by W. H. Hall.

General discussion.

Junior Normal Class, conducted by Miss Frances Walkley.

11:00—LECTURE. Rev. H. Frank Rall, Ph. D., "Paul and His Work."

### AFTERNOON.

1:30—WOMAN'S HOUR. Topic, "Adulteration of Food." Discussion conducted by Mrs. V. E. Keeler.

4:00—CHAUTAUQUA ROUND TABLE. "How and Why Encourage Popular Education in the community where we live. Short address by W. H. Hall. General discussion C. L. S. C. Council.

5:00—ASSEMBLY CHORUS DRILL. Conducted by George Waldo Lackey.

### EVENING.

7:30—MUSIC.

8:00—STEREOPTICON LECTURE. "Historic India, Ancient and Modern." Mrs. Mary Scott Badley.

### Rev. O. P. Gifford, D. D.

Rev. O. P. Gifford,
D. D.

Dr. Gifford is the popular pastor of the Delaware Avenue Baptist Church, Buffalo, New York. Without doubt he is one of the best speakers in his denomination, forcible, clear, and logical in all of his utterances. His addresses are full of that quaint wit and humor that make him at once popular with his audience. His earnest sympathy with young people and their work makes it very fitting that he should be the prominent speaker upon "Young People's Day." The *Buffalo Express* speaks of him as "Possessing the sturdiness of New England hills, the grace of New England training, the energy and touch with men and measures gained from contact and association with Boston, Chicago and Buffalo life. Dr. Gifford stands pre-eminent as a platform and pulpit orator."

### Rev. J. B. McLean

Prof. McLean is principal of the McLean Seminary at Simsbury and is a man of recognized ability upon the platform. His lecture will treat of the phenomena of instinct in the animal world, and that which simulates it very closely in vegetation, and the activities of inanimate matter. The argument will be to show by many illustrations that no hypothesis which eliminates the present active intelligence of a Universe Ruler can account for the happenings of the most familiar things which surround us.

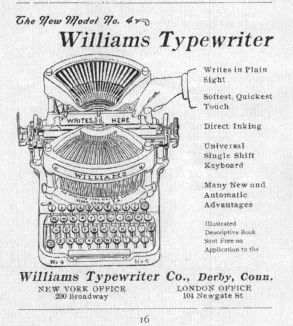

# Tuesday, July 30

---

*YOUNG PEOPLE'S DAY.*

---

MORNING.

8:30—CHAPEL SERVICE. Rev. J. P. Wagner.

9:00—CHAUTAUQUA NORMAL CLASS. V. "The Land of Palestine." Dr. J. L. Hurlbut.

Junior Chorus Drill, conducted by Mr. Lackey.

10:00—CHURCH CONGRESS. Fifth Session. Topic, "Young People's Societies, a Help or a Hindrance to the Church?" Address by Rev. Burdette B. Brown.

General discussion.

Junior Normal Class, conducted by Miss Frances Walkley.

11:00—LECTURE. "The Wisdom of Little Wits and What it Teaches Us." Rev. J. B. McLean, D .D.

AFTERNOON.

1:30—WOMAN'S HOUR. Topic, "Markets and Living in Other Lands." Discussion conducted by Mrs. V. E. Keeler.

2:30—MUSIC.

Platform Meeting in the interests of Young People's Societies, Rev. Burdette B. Brown presiding.

LECTURE. "The Problem of Life." Rev. O. P. Gifford, D .D.

4:00—CHAUTAUQUA ROUND TABLE. General Discussion on "The Books We Read," and "How to Start a Chautauqua Circle." C. L. S. C. Council.

5:00—ASSEMBLY CHORUS DRILL. Conducted by George Waldo Lackey

EVENING.

8:00—GRAND CONCERT.

### The Recognition Service

This is the first Recognition Day service ever held in Connecticut, and will afford opportunity for many graduate Chautauquans to pass through the golden gates and beneath the flower strewn arches which represent the triumphal completion of the Chautauqua course of Reading. The beautiful and impressive ritualistic service will be the same as that used at Chautauqua every year. The graduates of all past classes that have never passed the gates and arches will be given the privilege here. The members of the class of 1901 should inform Miss Kate F. Kimball at the Chautauqua offices, Cleveland, Ohio, that they desire to receive their diplomas at this Assembly. The undergraduates are expected to join in the procession. The C. L. S. C. Reception that follows the Recognition service is open to Chautauquans only and will be very informal and afford an opportunity for Chautauquans to become acquainted with each other. Music, short speeches and light refreshments will constitute the program. Mr. James A. Howarth, President of the New Haven Chautauqua Union, will preside during the speech-making.

"The Twentieth Century" is the name of the class that graduates this year. Its motto is "Light, Love, Life." The class flower is the "Coreopsis." A Recognition Day service is not complete without many flowers and it is hoped that they will be supplied in abundance by Chautauquans and their friends.

# Wednesday, July 31

*RECOGNITION DAY.*

MORNING.

8:30—CHAPEL SERVICE. Conducted by Rev W. F. Sheldon.

9:00—CHAUTAUQUA NORMAL CLASS. VI. "The Temple in the Time of Christ." Dr. J. L. Hurlbut.
Junior Chorus Drill, conducted by Mr. Lackey.

10:00—CHURCH CONGRESS. Sixth Session. Topic, "Some things I would aim to do if I were a minister." Address by Chas. A. Baldwin. "Some things I would try to do if I were a layman." Address by Rev. C. G. Clarke.

General discussion.

Junior Normal Class, conducted by Miss Frances Walkley.

11:00—LECTURE: "The New Woman of the Orient." Mrs. Mary Scott Badley.

AFTERNOON.

1:30—WOMAN'S HOUR. Topic, "Household Economics in the Public Schools." Discussion conducted by Mrs. V. E. Keeler.

2:00—CHAUTAUQUA PROCESSION. Band, Flower Girls, Assembly Officers, Chautauqua Graduates, Undergraduates, Class of 1901.

2:30—Passage Through the Golden Gate and Arches. Recognition Services. Music.

3:00—RECOGNITION DAY ADDRESS. Rev. Jesse Lyman Hurlbut, D. D.

Awarding diplomas to Class of 1901.

4:00—CHAUTAUQUA RECEPTION. For members of the C. L. S. C. alone, at which officers of the Assembly C. L. S. C. Association will be elected for the coming year.

4:30—Junior Concert under the direction of Mr. Lackey.

EVENING.

7:30—MUSIC.

8:00—STEREOPTICON LECTURE. "Beautiful India; Himalayan Scenery." Mrs. Mary Scott Badley.

THE NEW HAVEN DISTRICT CAMP MEETING WILL HOLD ITS THIRTY-SIXTH SESSION ON THESE GROUNDS AUGUST 2-12, INCLUSIVE. For programs apply to Rev. J. E. Adams, D. D., New Haven, Conn.

## How to Reach the Assembly

The stations, Plainville and Forestville on the N. Y., N. H. and H. Railway, are but a short distance from the grounds. Carriages will meet trains and transport passengers and luggage. The 'bus fare from Plainville will be 20 cents; from Forestville 10 cents. Those coming from the direction of Waterbury or Hartford will find it most convenient to leave the cars at Forestville. Round trip tickets may be purchased from July 23, good until August 12, at following rates:

## To Plainville Camp Station, or Forestville, and Return

| | |
|---|---|
| Ansonia, via Waterbury | $1.10 |
| Berlin, via New Britain | .30 |
| Danbury | 1.50 |
| East Derby, via Waterbury | 1.20 |
| Hartford | .50 |
| Higganum, via New Britain | .85 |
| Meriden | .55 |
| Middletown, via New Britain | .60 |
| Naugatuck, via Waterbury | .75 |
| New Britain | .30 |
| Pomperaug Valley | 1.05 |
| Springfield, via Hartford | 1.30 |
| Southford | .95 |
| Seymour, via Waterbury | 1.00 |
| Terryville | .30 |
| Torrington, via Waterbury | 1.20 |
| Waterbury, Meadow St. | .60 |
| Willimantic | 1.45 |
| Winsted, via Waterbury | 1.45 |
| Vernon | .85 |
| Melrose | 1.00 |
| New Milford, via Hawleyville | 1.70 |

## To Plainville and Return

| | |
|---|---|
| Avon | .30 |
| Bridgeport, via New Haven | 1.35 |
| Cheshire | .40 |
| Collinsville | .40 |
| Granby | .60 |
| Mt. Carmel | .60 |
| Plantsville | .30 |
| New Haven | .85 |
| Simsbury | .45 |
| South Norwalk | 1.80 |
| Wallingford, via New Haven | 1.20 |
| Westfield, Mass. | 1.05 |
| New London, via New Haven | 2.40 |
| Saybrook, via New Haven | 1.85 |
| Unionville | .30 |
| New Hartford | .55 |

If your station is not in the above list and you purchase a full fare ticket to the Assembly, you will there be furnished with a ticket by the R. R. Secretary, Rev. H. C. Whitney, which will entitle you to purchase and return upon a one-half fare ticket. No excursion tickets will be accepted upon the third rail electric trains.

## Accommodations

There are over one hundred cottages upon the grounds, many of which will be open to lodgers, and there will be no lack of accommodations to those who wish to stay the entire session or a few days. Some accommodations are better furnished than others. It is always safest to bring your own towels, hand-glass and toilet articles. Upon reaching the grounds application should be made at once at the Association Building, where a list of lodgings and prices will always be kept. The prices will range from 25 cents a night to $3.00 a week for furnished rooms. Further information as to board lodging, etc., may be obtained from Rev. Geo. M. Brown, Derby, Conn.

The Association owns no tents, but parties that can furnish their own tents will find delightful locations for living this way in the woods. By this method a neighborhood party can have a very pleasant outing at small expense. Grocery, ice, and milk wagons visit the grounds every day providing supplies at the usual market prices.

Have letters directed: "Assembly Grounds, Plainville, Conn." Inquire for and mail letters at the Secretary's office. Stationery and postage can be obtained at the office.

## The Entrance Fee

The Assembly management introduces this year a new method for defraying the expenses of the program. Heretofore no gate fee has ever been asked, but collections have been taken at every service. This year there will be a nominal entrance fee, but no collections. This is the universal custom at Chautauqua Assemblies and has been found to be the only fair way of meeting the expenses. The management is absolutely positive that there will not be offered at any assembly this year as good a program for such a small entrance fee as is charged at the gates of the Connecticut Chautauqua Assembly.

## Tickets

SEASON TICKET $1.00. This ticket is good for every session of the Assembly and for entrance and exit to and from the grounds at any time. It must bear the name of the owner, and be shown at request of the gatekeeper.

DAY TICKET 25 CENTS. This ticket is good for all the sessions of one day only, and for entrance and exit at any time during that day.

MORNING TICKET 10 CENTS. This ticket is good for the morning session only, the date of which is stamped upon the back of the ticket.

MORNING AND AFTERNOON TICKET 20 CENTS. This ticket is good for one morning and afternoon session only, the date of which is stamped upon the back.

AFTERNOON TICKET 15 CENTS. This ticket is good for one afternoon session only, the date of which is stamped upon the back.

AFTERNOON AND EVENING TICKET 20 CENTS. This ticket is good for one afternoon and evening session only, the date of which is stamped upon the back.

EVENING TICKET 15 CENTS. This ticket is good for one evening session only, the date of which is stamped upon the back.

CHILDREN under 12 years of age admitted free.

READ YOUR TICKET CAREFULLY as soon as purchased, and by kindly following its directions you will save trouble and confusion to all concerned. All persons on the grounds must be provided with tickets.

## Music at the Assembly

One of the most enjoyable attractions of the program will be the music it offers. The chorus should have the loyal support of everybody who can sing. Solo, quartette and orchestral numbers will be given before lectures and entertainments. The three concerts will be first class in every particular. The Plainville Military Band, one of the three best in the state, will furnish music upon several occasions. Miss Josephine Hansen of Shelton will be present for a number of days. For the past three years she has been the soprano soloist of St. James Episcopal Church, Derby. She interprets English song from ballads to the "Rejoice Greatly," in "The Messiah," and is also equally able to execute coloratura music like Richard Strauss' "Spring Time Waltz."

Miss Maud Marvin of Torrington will be at the Assembly the last three days of the session. She is a singer of much popularity and is equally at home in church concert or oratorio work. She has a rich contralto voice which has won her much praise for its flexibility and growing power. She is the contralto soloist at Trinity Episcopal Church, Waterbury. Other noted singers will be present and assist in solo and concert work.

80

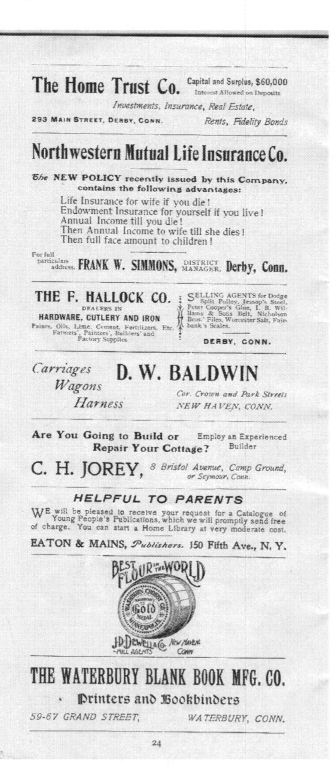

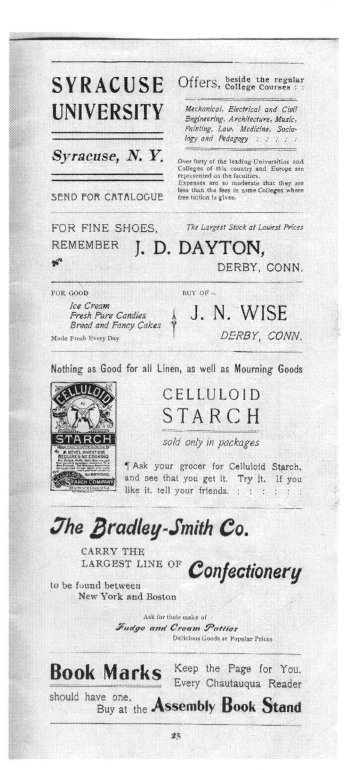

# A Corset That Cannot Break at the Waist ⌒

It matters not what the style of the corset is, or what it is made of, if it breaks at the waist line it is rendered uncomfortable and useless.

"Cannot Break at the Waist"

## The Cresco Corset

Is disconnected in front at the waist line, and has elastic gores at each side, so it CANNOT BREAK AT THE WAIST. Suit. ble for any day and all the day. Good to work in, walk in or rest in. It is shapely, comfortable and durable, and as it cannot break at the waist, it is the CHEAPEST CORSET A LADY CAN BUY.

Where the CRESCO is not kept by dealers it will be sent postpaid for

### $1.00

*Reduced Prices to Ministers' Families*

SUMMER AND WHITE OR DRAB JEAN, LONG, SHORT OR MEDIUM LENGTH.

## The Michigan Corset Co., Jackson, Mich.

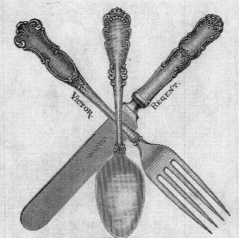

## Chapter Six:  Evolution from Spiritual to Social

### Good-Bye

*Small white cottages in the forest,*
*Rustling trees in sunlight shine,*
*Many friends to greet us daily,*
*Good-bye, 'till next summer time.*

*Busy-days have gone before us,*
*Now the autumn time is here,*
*Take our quilts and turn us homeward,*
*Good-bye, 'till another year.*

*(Place setting keepsake at 1934*
*woman's guild last lunch of season)*

The Methodist Camp Grounds at Plainville continued to thrive during the first half of the 20th century, adapting to the times with expanded recreation facilities for youth, use of movies in its programs (a projector platform may still be seen today in the auditorium) and better accommodation for the automobile.

Methodism during this period also became more staid and institutionalized, becoming one of the largest organized religious bodies in the country.  Evangelical zeal began to take a back seat as large sophisticated Methodist churches with huge physical plants including gymnasiums and bowling alleys emerged.

While newspaper accounts as late as the 1940s listed as many as 2,000 persons in attendance at the camp grounds for Sunday service, it was obvious that the camp meeting itself was on the decline. Response to the Gospel was less and less emotional and more and more intellectual.

Many private cottage owners, descendents of the founders, together with new folk with no ties to Methodism and some to no religious expression, began to spend entire summers on the grounds. These changes are reflected in the formation of the woman's guild.

In 1933 a group of women interested in quilts and community through fellowship began meeting at the camp grounds to work on quilts, exchange patterns, and discuss the possibility of a quilt exhibit. On a rainy July 25, 1934, the first exhibit of 23 quilts together with hooked, braided, and crochet rugs took place. Following the success of this exhibit, the club, meeting every week, committed to assist the camp grounds financially and continued their work as the Camp Ground Quilt Club.

In the depression year of 1934, Miss Rose Beebe offered to piece a quilt top and put on it the names of people who had a connection to the camp grounds, living and deceased. Over 1,000 names were secured and the following year Miss Beebe presented $100 earned from the quilt to the Trustees who used the funds toward the screening of the auditorium. This quilt is on display today at the Plainville Historical Society.

In the following years the club began raising money to refurbish the association building and to support the music ministries and library of the campground.

At the club's meetings Susan Henderson, known affectionately as Grandma Henderson, began giving inspirational talks characterized by words of encouragement and hope in living. Upon her death in 1938 the name of this group was changed to the Susan Henderson Memorial Guild and included 50 members. Although quilt making gradually vanished as well as the memorialized name, the group continues today with its socializing (trips to casinos, pot luck suppers, and tag sales) as well as its benefactor work for the camp grounds.

In the woman's guild history one can clearly see the wane of Methodism and the emergence of a social summer community at Plainville.

Susan "Grandma" Henderson.

Conn. Chautauqua building as it appears today. Built in 1893 for First Church Hartford, it was purchased by Chautauqua Inc. in 1921 and used until 1970 when it became the arts and crafts building of the Plainville Campgrounds Association, eventually surrendering to vacancy and raccoons. It was privately purchased and renovated with the coming of sewers in 1992-1993.

The *Much Room* or "Mushroom" cottage as it appears today. Built by Gay Sheldon on a deeded tent lot in 1913 for Harriet A. Barrett to accommodate her large family, she gave it the name *Much Room*. Later it became known as the *Mushroom* cottage for its whimsical porch that mimicked the profusion of mushrooms that grew on the grounds.

Harriet Barrett on the porch of the *Much Room* cottage with her growing family.

## Chapter Seven: The Plainville Camp Ground Association

On Wednesday, June 20, 1956, beginning with a hymn sing, the New Haven District Camp Grounds held their annual meeting in the auditorium with a larger than usual crowd present. It was a difficult meeting for all.

Transcribed minutes reflect that the camp grounds were in decline. Churches who owned cottages were not paying annual fees and many had turned their cottages back to the association. Privately owned cottages were paying most of the income. For that year there were only three "religious meetings" sponsored by the Methodists. There were numerous complaints about decline and lack of interest. There had been little response to mailings and posters.

One minister summed up the frustration well: "It is the Compounce Amusement Park and the race track we are trying to get away from. We are trying to develop a lot different taste for our young people and for that reason these grounds are not suitable for a camp. The fact of the matter is that changes have taken place in church life. We did not have automobiles, movies and TV; people now do not want to go to church more than once on Sunday morning. I have done every thing I can to drag people over here. I can understand how cottage owners love the place, but we have to meet the competition of this generation in ways that are effective."

This minister was speaking to a request from the Methodist Training Center Corporation of the New York East Conference that consideration be given to the sale of the Plainville Camp Ground and the proceeds be used to help purchase a large and more useable campsite for use of the young people and members of the Methodist Church.

When this request was put to motion the discussion was rather volitile with heated exchange between the clergy and private cottage owners. In reality it was the private cottage owners who were providing the largest amount of financial support and improvements and doing so without much representation. The cottage owners leased the land on which their cottages stood, and control of the grounds lay in the hands of the Methodist church.

After much discussion, a committee of ten was formed to come up with a method of selling the camp grounds. By July 20, 1957, 69 cottage owners, 12 churches and Chautauqua (owning 82 buildings in all) had formed themselves into a "religious organization" known as the Plainville Camp Ground Association Inc. and filed papers. Temporary officers had been installed and each cottage owner was given one vote. Some of these individuals were Protestant evangelicals who wanted to maintain the spiritual lifestyle and program of the founders. Others were newcomers who were not interested in spirituality but desired a vacation home in the country. (In 1956 the area was as yet undeveloped.)

At a meeting of this new organization members voted to accept the offer of the Methodist Church to sell the campgrounds to them for the sum of $14,000, payments of which were to be made over five years.  Bylaws were drawn up and adopted on Aug 3, 1957.  These are the same ones operative today albeit with many alterations.

Over the course of the next few years the Plainville Chautauqua disbanded, the remaining churches pulled out, and several cottages fell into ruin and were torn down.  There were many threats to the new organization's existence, however there were also several stabilizing forces.

One of these was the Forestville Bible Conference, which through the early 1980s continued to hold an annual conference week that included Bible study, worship services, and fellowship.  The conference was essentially a week of vacation in an evangelical Christian setting. The speaker for the week boarded in one of the cottages.  Families could rent a cottage for the week, and there was meal service in the John Wesley Dining Hall. Several members of this group owned cottages and served on the board, and they continued to make the grounds a mecca for the Protestant evangelical.

Another stabilizing influence was the fact that members of the new association renovated the cottage on the circle formerly owned by the East Pearl Street Methodist Church of New Haven and began to hold Sunday services and other religious events there.  This Chapel was named for Captain John Marvin Parker of Old Lyme, Connecticut, who had served for 41 years as secretary of the Methodist Camp Grounds.  Sunday afternoon services are still held in this quaint chapel that reflects the only remaining spiritual symbol of the grounds, the auditorium having been converted into a picnic pavilion.  The bylaws state that the

"Parker Memorial Chapel is the physical and spiritual center for the association. It is expected that only those who wish to uphold the traditions laid down by its founders as embodied in the chapel will become members of the association."

The Forestville Bible Conference and the Chapel services were important influences that held the association together through a number of threats.

# Chapter Eight: Threat and Revival

In the years that followed the formation of the Plainville Camp Ground Association, the farms across Camp Street in Bristol succumbed to the development of numerous housing units. Northwest Drive was cut through the southern portion of the grounds. Fortunately, the town constructed two schools to the east on large, well-landscaped tracts of land and there was enough wooded area to protect the grounds from the developments to the north. (Site of the spring and Bethel)

Noise pollution, at least in the daylight hours, destroyed the quiet as vehicular traffic increased dramatically due to the development of Route 6 and the urbanization of the entire region. This resulted in road widening and the installation of traffic lights on Camp Street.

When sewers were installed in 1969, only the dining hall was hooked up. Individual cottages retained their cesspools or no facilities. Communal toilets and showers were still in operation, a large septic system having been installed for them. This situation rendered a number of cottages unsellable and uninhabitable.

In March of 1966, the camp ground was labeled as a "pocket of deterioration" and earmarked for a $547,900 urban renewal project. Fortunately, Plainville became more interested in developing its town center and the project was put on the back burner.

In 1967, however, zoning officials moved to condemn the entire grounds due to faulty electrical wiring. This pending action occurred at the same time that the association was considering a major proposal to develop the grounds for elderly housing.

Called by some "Tobacco Road," the grounds exuded an air of abandonment and decline.

The fiscal state of the association however was good despite extremely modest annual fees (today they still run only three figures). And of course there was the commitment of the cottage owners and the spiritual core. This combination enabled these challenges to be met and by the 1980s a development occurred that enabled the physical grounds to be put on a path that would preserve them for future generations.

These were the days of the country's emerging historic preservation movement. A number of older members of the association were in tune with that movement and on May 19, 1980, the grounds under their original name, the New Haven District Camp Ground, Plainville, was placed on the National Register of Historic Places as a significant resource in American history, architecture, archaeology and culture that merited preservation.

While the stipulation was merely honorary, the association board wonderfully misinterpreted the honor (as it does to this day), believing that the recognition meant that exteriors of buildings could not be altered. They in turn wrote this rule into their bylaws, assuring the preservation of the grounds' remarkable architectural resources and history.

Around the same time period, the grounds were discovered by a group of people with a bent to the appreciation of historic ambiance and who felt it was a very reasonable place to live seasonally. These were mostly younger retirees who sought to spend winters in Florida or elsewhere and summers in Connecticut. These folks began to buy, restore and resell cottages to like-minded individuals always retaining one for themselves. They also became active in the business affairs of the association establishing strong bylaws with strict rules for property maintenance.

Within time, sewers, new water lines, and lighting were installed. This, combined with a more intentional stewardship of association buildings, brought the camp grounds to the remarkable state of preservation it is in today. Indeed so well has the progression been that if the non-profit mission of the grounds as a religious organization were to suffer demise, historic preservation could well substitute as that mission, completing the transition from sacred to secular.

Cottages today typically sell in the five-figure range. For the most part they require constant maintenance. Admission to the association and thus ownership, is non-discriminatory with a pledge to abide by the rather strict bylaws, and a symbolic pledge to abide by the principles of the founders as embodied in the Chapel. Land on which the cottages stand is leased and only seasonal occupancy is allowed (May through October). In essence it is a seasonal residential community committed to preserving its place in America's architectural history with limited connections to its own religious and cultural history.

The Caretakers House, home of the resident overseer of the grounds year round. A bit altered, the house and stable still stand today.

Leon Gaylord Sheldon and his wife Margaret demonstrating the patriotism that reigned in the country following the Civil War and Reconstruction.

Gay Sheldon was a craftsman who built at least two cottages on the grounds as well as the auditorium pulpit, table, and clock.

The Sheldons were responsible for decorating the platform for the Camp Meeting week.

The Gables (1910)

Cottage of Gay and Eva Sheldon

The birdhouse was an exact replica of the Kensington Methodist Church. Gay Sheldon was not only the builder of this, his own cottage, but the *Much Room* or *Mushroom* cottage as well. Both still stand today.

The Glad Inn (Leon Gladding family on porch)

Leon Gladding was caretaker of the grounds for many years and built the Glad Inn shown here. In the early days of the camp ground, Gladding was responsible for many improvements including the children's playground and stone bridge, the stone bridge and path to Mt. Olivet and several other stonewalls still seen today. Note the Chinese paper lanterns on the porch. This was in the tradition of "illumination night" (adopted from Oak Bluffs), when the entire grounds were illuminated by ornate Chinese lanterns inviting all to stroll the beautifully illuminated grounds. The tradition continues at Oak Bluffs to this day using electricity. The custom was discontinued at Plainville for fear of fire.

The period between 1890-1912 was a time of great nationalism, the country having recently emerged from the Civil War and Reconstruction, when it sought unity through patriotism. Photographs of the grounds of the time show them profusely adorned with bunting and flags.

The athletic field, on the opposite side of Camp Street, was purchased in 1913 for $300. This five acre parcel was sold to the Lutheran Church in 1958. Legend has it that the day before the sale the great tree to the left was struck by lightning! The view of the Bristol hills and stone walls was the buena vista from the camp grounds.

The athletic field was the site of
many a camp fire and ball game!

Pleasant View cottage, owned by Ulysses S. Clark, shown here in an early photo. This cottage was pre-fabricated in West Haven. Mr. Clark was responsible for the stone wall around his cottage which still stands today. The white stones in the wall were gathered by his son Donald from the beach at Savin Rock in West Haven.

Edna Richardson (1896)
Mrs. Ulysses S. Clark

The Clark cottage today. While most of the cottages have maintained their integrity, several like this one have been adapted for modern use without concern for historic preservation.

The only known remaining camp ground lantern that illuminated the grounds at night. These lamps hung on trees and were lit just before dark and extinguished at 10 p.m. Electricity arrived on the grounds in 1913.

Through the 20th Century many cottages succumbed to the elements or neglect such as the one pictured here. Note lantern on tree at right.

Leisure was the name of the game for these Bristol
Ave. cottage owners. These tranquil hammocks
today would not be as pleasant with hundreds of cars
whizzing by on Camp St. The grounds were marketed
in the first half of the 20th Century as the "coolest
place in the state!"

Above: Interior of
the Parker Memorial
Chapel today.

Right: Original pulpit
and platform table of
the tabernacle or
auditorium. In the
first half of the 20th
Century this furniture
was fashioned from
native sumac by
Leon "Gay" Sheldon.

## *Forestville Summer Mornings*
## *Folksong by Daniel Rausch - 1981*

*Woke up this morning to a pouring rain*
*And it nurtured all my thoughts again*
*Of childhood-time vacations in the woods.*
*When the early morning rain would begin*
*To dance on our cottage's roof of tin*
*I'd drowsily awake to a sound so good.*

> *Oh, Forestville morning,*
> *I didn't realize that you taught my mind to see -*
> *Oh, when Summer starts to slip away,*
> *The Forestville Summer mornings shine in my memory.*

*Soon the rain would stop and the sun come out*
*People in the village are up and about,*
*They're doing their shopping and the lawns are being mowed.*
*There's a blue jay squawking in a hemlock tree,*
*He's a beauty of Nature with a voice so free,*
*As you walk don't you see the flowers blooming on the side of the road?*

> *Oh, Forestville morning,*
> *It comes as no surprise that you taught my mind to see -*
> *Oh, when Autumn days turn dark and gray,*
> *The Forestville Summer mornings shine in my memory.*

*Long shadows point to the twilight hours*
*And it's rest for the trees and the birds and flowers,*
*I begin to see the rising of the yellow moon.*
*The tea kettle's boiling on the old wood stove,*
*All God's children are blessed with love -*
*At the old piano I play an old hymn tune.*

> *Oh, Forestville Morning,*
> *When morning gilds the skies that's when you taught my mind*
> *to see -*
> *Oh, when Winter snows seem here to stay,*
> *The Forestville Summer mornings shine in my memory.*

Unaltered interior of a cottage on the Circle. While association bylaws prohibit exterior changes, owners have free reign in the interiors. While some have been redone as "Victorian" cottages, some have succumbed to renovations inappropriate to the period and purpose of original construction.

# Epilogue

If one visits the Plainville Camp Grounds today and walks into the circle, one is dumbstruck by its time warp. Here, as I mentioned in the introduction, the air seems hallowed by the breath of other times. It is not hard to imagine hundreds of people gathered in the great tabernacle with hundreds more on the porches of the cottages. One can almost hear again the great hymns wafting on the air, the orations of famous speakers, the orchestral music of Chautauqua, or the shouts of individuals propelled into a new life of purpose and service to others.

In the evening, when the Camp Street traffic is stilled, one is tranquilized by a mighty chorus of katydids, and the heart is once again strangely warmed by this place that gave respite to those gone before and continues to do so for us today.

# Acknowledgements

This volume has been a good 15 years in the making and over these years many people have contributed to it in various ways.

I was urged to write it some 15 years ago by Betty Antonelli, then Association president. Betty and her husband Andy have worked tirelessly to save the Camp Ground and to bring it to a continuing sense of community.

There are few, if any, footnotes or credits in this volume. Simply put, many of my facts come either through the oral tradition, from the Camp Ground records, or were stored over the years in my journalistic head. The spirit of those recollections were reinforced by Captain John Marvin Parker's brief history of the grounds, Harriet Eaton's history, oral stories of Nathalie Munroe, and written reminiscences done in the 1970s and 1980s by Ruth Reynolds Carmical, Winifred Bowler, and Dorothy Young. Esther Pope provided distinct memories of summers at the ground in the 1950s and 1960s.

Sarah Zimmerman's National Register of historic Places Inventory Nomination Form for the Camp Grounds was also invaluable.

While many of the photographs, postcards and other ephemera are from my personal collection or that of Harriet Eaton, I will ever be grateful to Tom Dickau of Bristol, Conn., for sharing his extensive Forestville postcard collection and allowing me the free use of it here. I look

forward to his forthcoming book on the town of
Forestville. Various other photos and prints are
from the Billy Graham Center Museum,
Chautauqua Institute Archives, and *The Gospel in
Hymns* (New York; Charles Scribner's Sons, 1954).

This has not been an inexpensive venture,
but many headaches and hundreds of dollars were
saved by my extraordinary daughter-in-law, Estelle
Paskausky Pope, a librarian at Yale University,
who assumed the responsibility of the book's entire
layout. Esther Pope, Ethan Pope, and James
Killian were invaluable proofreaders.

## About the Author

During his lifetime Arthur Pope has enjoyed
long careers in the Congregational ministry and his
avocations of historic preservation, antiques, social
justice and journalism. He and his wife Esther
reside in Connecticut and enjoy spending time at
their Simsbury Church Cottage at Forestville.

Printed in the United States
By Bookmasters